Beyond the Bowl

the Cereal Lover's Ultimate Cookbook

DEBBY MAUGANS

CB

CONTEMPORARY BOOKS

Library of Congress Cataloging-in-Publication Data

Maugans, Debby.
    Beyond the bowl : the cereal lover's ultimate cookbook / Debby
Maugans.
        p.   cm.
    Includes index.
    ISBN 0-8092-3005-4
    1. Cookery (Cereals).   I. Title.
TX808.M3697   1997
641.331—dc21
                                      97-22433
                                          CIP

For my Jessie Kate,
who puts the snap, crackle, and pop into my life

Cover design by Monica Baziuk
Cover illustration copyright © Brian Battles
Cover photograph by Sharon Hoogstraten
Interior design by Nancy Freeborn
Interior illustrations by Lana Mullen

Published by Contemporary Books
An imprint of NTC/Contemporary Publishing Company
4255 West Touhy Avenue, Lincolnwood (Chicago), Illinois 60646-1975 U.S.A.
Copyright © 1997 by Debby Maugans
Manufactured in the United States of America
International Standard Book Number: 0-8092-3005-4
16   15   14   13   12   11   10   9   8   7   6   5   4   3   2

CONTENTS

ACKNOWLEDGMENTS

Many thanks to the family and friends who have crunched their way through countless boxes of cereal: To Mom and Dad for tasting more cereal dishes than they ever dreamed of, and for making some of these recipes even better with their suggestions. To Dean Nakos for freeing me from the confines of butter and Worcestershire sauce to create snack mixes I want to eat by the gallon. And to the gang at Vision Industries—Deryl Duer, George Fowler, and John Fleming—for holding my hand through my "computer breakdown" as well as spending hours perfecting cereal photography and being cheerleaders. I greatly appreciate the generosity of Marcia Mogelonsky in her sharing of cereal trivia. Thanks to my agent, Alice Martell, for having the wit to grab on to an unorthodox book like this one. Finally, I greatly respect Wendy Hubbert's energetic determination to guide me to do it right, and I admire and appreciate her clever humor.

INTRODUCTION

Cereal Lovers, Unite!

I AM A CEREAL FIEND. I eat cereal all day long and into the wee hours. And I'm far from alone: when I decided to confess my addiction in the form of this book, friends, acquaintances, colleagues, and people I met in bars came out of the closet about their cereal habits. One male friend owned up to eating Cap'n Crunch during the Super Bowl until the roof of his mouth hurt. Others 'fessed up to keeping nothing in the fridge but cereal, milk, and beer. A woman I met at the health club said that no matter what time of day or night she comes home from a trip, she goes straight to the kitchen and pours a bowl of Cocoa Puffs. The favorite meal of one award-winning chef I know: you guessed it, cereal.

I became addicted to crunching in college, with those little boxes of Cheerios and Trix and individual cups of ice cream smuggled out of the cafeteria. I'd eat Cheerios with ice cream on it for breakfast so I could skip the dining hall and sleep a little later before class. Trix sustained me through many a late-night cram session. To this day, the sound of cereal crunching in my mouth keeps me alert and thinking clearly while I work.

I've since gone through many cereal fetishes. Nowadays, the first thing I do in the morning is crush Nabisco Shredded Wheat in a large café au lait cup, then add a package of sweetener and just enough milk (or chocolate milk, if we have it) to reach the top of the cereal. It goes into the refrigerator to get soggy while I put on coffee and my face, feed the cat, and wake up my daughter. I eat Toasted Oatmeal Squares dipped one at a time in fat-free cream cheese while I watch the six o'clock news and cook dinner (if dinner is something hot and not cereal). At night I munch on popcorn mixed with Corn Pops. I store opened cereal boxes in the refrigerator—chilling makes cereal stay crisper longer no matter what I pour on it. The day a new brand of cereal goes on the market, you can bet it'll be on my shelf.

You're probably picking up this book because you, too, could eat literally nothing but cereal for breakfast, lunch, and dinner. *Beyond the Bowl* will show you how to do just that—with practically every brand and kind of cereal there is. From "Things to Eat While You're Making Them" in Chapter 1 to decadent desserts in Chapter 9, "The Icing on the Cereal," I've turned cereal into fabulous cookies, nifty appetizers, irresistible breads, breakfast ideas extraordinaire, outrageous snacks, even main dishes.

How to Use This Book

You can use this book by chapters, or, to make it easy to find a recipe that uses your personal favorite cereal or one that you already have on the shelf, turn to the Recipe Reference List and look for the brand and type. For instance, if you have a box of Post Fruit & Fibre cereal and want to know what foods you can make with it, go to the back of the book and look up Post Fruit & Fibre for recipe listings and page numbers. You can browse through the recipe names at the beginning of each chapter, or go to the standard recipe index on page 205.

Within the chapters you'll find recipes organized by the shape of the cereal used in them: *flakes* (cornflakes, bran flakes), *shreds* (such as shredded wheat cereals), *squares* (such as Chex cereals), and *"the good stuff"* (flaky, fruity, crunchy nugget, full-of-fiber cereals such as granolas, Grape-Nuts, and cereals that strive to keep up with the FDA's food pyramid by adding fruits and nuts to whole-grain flakes).

■ Flakes make terrific crunchy coatings for baked and fried seafood and chicken. Finely crushed flakes can be partially substituted for flour in breads and sweets. And used instead of bread crumbs, crushed flakes become tasty binding agents in crab cakes, meat loaf, meatballs, and burgers—without making the food heavy.

■ Shreds add lots of texture, but the flavor is not overpowering. You can make stuffings and fantastic breads and muffins, or take a cue from Mediterranean cooks and make delicious pastries.

- Chunky square cereals were born to stay crisp in milk, so they're perfect in any recipe where crunch is needed. Great in nachos instead of corn chips.

- "The good stuff" adds healthy things to breads, desserts, and main dishes. The best carrot cake I've ever tasted is in the chapter "For Kids Only," and it's made with Kellogg's Müeslix Raisin & Almond Crunch with Dates. Look for these recipes with a healthier slant in every chapter.

Each recipe will work with a range of specific cereals, which I've listed at the beginning, so you'll find it easy to substitute your favorites or make that disappointing new cereal into something more appetizing. Note that some recipes will work with two or more different cereal shapes, so they won't be grouped within a shape category: for instance, in Pucker Up Lemon Squares (page 29), you could use Rice Krispies, Waffle Crisp, or Kix. Magic Chocolate Cereal Bars (page 28) use granola *and* squares. You'll find miscellaneous shapes like crisps and Os sprinkled throughout, and all those fabulous sticky-sweet junk-food cereals are in "The Icing on the Cereal."

■ ■ ■

This book of cereal is a tribute to all of us who thrive on the boxed stuff. And with 215 ways to eat it, the kitchen beckons. Break out a fresh box of Golden Grahams, grab a spatula, and dig in!

Quick Fixes

Things to Eat While You're Making Them

60-Second Recipes

5-Minute Recipes

Banana Crunch Pudding

10-Minute Recipes

Chocolate Ice-Cream Cones
Chocolate Granola Fruit Drops

15-Minute Recipes

Easy Chocolate Crispy Bar
Bran-Nutty Cheese Balls
Quick Peanut Butter and Jelly Oatmeal Crisp Cookies
Aunt Cora's Special Cookies

THINGS TO EAT
WHILE YOU'RE MAKING THEM

- Roll spoonfuls of peanut butter in crushed Quaker Cap'n Crunch or Post Waffle Crisp. Or just dip a spoon into the jar and sprinkle with cereal.

- Spoon Ben & Jerry's Cherry Garcia Ice Cream into a glass cup; microwave on HIGH for 10 to 30 seconds, or until soft, then stir until melted. The slush should still be cool. Pour over Kellogg's Raisin Bran if you like instant mush or General Mills Crispy Wheats 'N Raisins if you want it to stay crispy longer.

- Dip Healthy Choice from Kellogg's Honey Wheat Squares into peanut butter or vanilla yogurt.

- Spoon whipped topping over Ralston Foods Cookie-Crisp, Quaker Cap'n Crunch Deep Sea Crunch, or Post Waffle Crisp in a bowl; top with sliced bananas or strawberries for a quick sundae when you're out of ice cream.

- Dip pretzels in peanut butter or melted chocolate and then in granola with or without fruit. Try: Kellogg's Low Fat Granola, General Mills Nature Valley Low Fat Fruit Granola, or Quaker 100% Natural Granola or Sun Country Granola.

- Top a Kellogg's Frosted Mini-Wheat with a teaspoon of cream cheese and then jam.

- Load up a bowl of cereal topped with

  spoonfuls of peanut butter and strawberry yogurt

  honey, raisins, and nuts

  frozen yogurt with apple butter or maple syrup

  cappuccino-flavored frozen yogurt and melted hazelnut-chocolate spread

  a frozen Eskimo Pie or 3 Musketeers bar, cut up, and cherries, if desired

  raspberries and hot fudge sauce

  vanilla fudge or strawberry frozen yogurt and frozen strawberries in syrup, thawed

  chopped Snickers bars or Reese's Peanut Butter Cups

60-SECOND RECIPES

- Roll ice-cream scoops in crushed Kellogg's Frosted Mini-Wheats or Nabisco Frosted Wheat Bites; store in the freezer until you need one. Top with chocolate sauce.

- Layer Jell-O, Post Fruity Pebbles, and thawed frozen whipped topping for an instant kid's dessert.

- For cereal mousse, fold together equal amounts of sweetened yogurt or instant pudding and thawed, frozen whipped topping, then add Ralston Foods Cookie-Crisp, Quaker Popeye Cocoa Blasts, Post Waffle Crisp, Kellogg's Frosted Cheerios, or any sweetened cereal of your choice.

- Mix together Kellogg's Pop-Tarts Crunch Frosted Brown Sugar Cinnamon or Cinnamon Mini Buns and chocolate-covered peanuts or raisins. Stir into softened ice cream and eat immediately or refreeze.

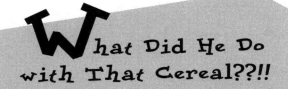

What Did He Do with That Cereal??!!

In one episode of *Seinfeld,* Kramer pours a bowl of cereal and leaves Jerry's apartment with it. Here's what I can't figure out: **Where did he go with it?** The movies? His apartment? Newman's apartment? Out for a walk? **What did he add to the bowl?** Nothing? Or possibly chocolate milk, popcorn, and hot sauce for a snack? French vanilla- or hazelnut-flavored coffee creamer? Coffee? Orange juice?

5-MINUTE RECIPES

■ Microwave chocolate morsels on MEDIUM for 30 seconds at a time or until you can stir until melted. Be sure to use a clean, dry glass bowl. Dip banana chunks in melted chocolate and roll in granola without fruit (Kellogg's Low Fat Granola without Raisins, Quaker Sun Country Granola with Almonds, or Quaker 100% Natural Granola Oats & Honey).

■ Load up a peanut butter sandwich with one of these: Kellogg's Low Fat Granola, Frosted Rice Krispies, Frosted Cheerios; Quaker Marshmallow Stars, 100% Natural Granola Oats & Honey, Sun Country Granola with Almonds, Cap'n Crunch; or Ralston Foods Cookie-Crisp. Press down on the bread to crush and mush. For a more civilized version, serve the sandwich open-faced on raisin bread toast or on a split bagel with cream cheese.

■ Dip strawberries in melted chocolate and roll in crushed sweetened cereal such as Kellogg's Frosted Flakes, Kellogg's Double Dip Crunch, Post Waffle Crisp, or Ralston Foods Cookie-Crisp.

Banana Crunch Pudding

Sugar-coated flakes of Post Banana Nut Crunch will not get soggy and will add more banana flavor. You can also use General Mills Cinnamon Toast Crunch or Kellogg's Double Dip Crunch.

> 2 (4-ounce) containers refrigerated vanilla pudding, or
> 1 cup prepared instant pudding
> 1 cup cereal
> 1 banana, sliced

1. Layer the pudding, cereal, and banana in 2 glasses.

2. Eat immediately.

Yield: 2 servings

10-MINUTE RECIPES

- Mix 2 tablespoons melted butter with 2 tablespoons steak sauce. Toss with 3 cups any Ralston Foods Chex cereal and spread in a 9-inch glass pie plate. Microwave on HIGH for 3 to 4 minutes, stirring and scraping the pie plate with a rubber spatula every 1½ minutes. Spread on paper towels to cool.

- Melt 2 tablespoons butter and 2 tablespoons hot pepper jelly and toss with any Ralston Foods Chex cereal before microwaving as above.

- For a quick fruit crisp: heat canned apple, cherry, or other pie filling, put in a bowl, and sprinkle with granola with or without fruit (Kellogg's Low Fat Granola, Quaker Sun Country Granola, Quaker 100% Natural Granola, or General Mills Nature Valley Low Fat Fruit Granola). Top with ice cream.

Chocolate Ice-Cream Cones

To make cones even better, place 12 ounces semisweet chocolate morsels in a deep glass bowl; microwave on HIGH 2 minutes, then stir until smooth. One at a time, dip the tops of 24 ice-cream cones in chocolate to a depth of 1 inch; roll to coat to a depth of 2 inches, if possible. Quickly remove each chocolate-coated cone and roll it in crushed Quaker Cap'n Crunch, Post Waffle Crisp, or Ralston Foods Cookie-Crisp. Place the cones upside down on waxed paper; let stand until the chocolate hardens. Store in an airtight container in the refrigerator.

Dorm Food

Any of the 5-Minute Recipes and 10-Minute Recipes can be accomplished with a hot pot or microwave in your room or dorm kitchenette. (Be sure to clean the hot pot before shoving it under the bed.) Grocery shopping will be cheaper if you sneak boxes of whatever cereal you can from the cafeteria. Here are a few more things to pilfer besides cereal, along with what to do with them.

- **cups of ice cream:** Stir cereal into them.
- **cartons of yogurt:** Eat yogurt on top of cereal and you can sleep through breakfast in the dining hall.
- **dishes of cobbler:** Top with granola for a healthy late-night snack.
- **brownies and packages of strawberry jam:** To make hockey-puck brownies appetizing, top them with one of those ice-cream cups, drizzle with strawberry jam, and sprinkle with cereal.
- **rolls, butter, jelly:** Make yourself a cereal sandwich.
- **chips:** Sprinkle granola on a chip and enjoy. Or break up chips and mix with cereal to satisfy your sweet and salty cravings at the same time.

Chocolate Granola Fruit Drops

Use granola without raisins because you're already adding dried fruit. Quaker Sun Country Granola with Almonds, Quaker 100% Natural Granola Oats & Honey, or Kellogg's Low Fat Granola without Raisins makes crunchy, fruity fudge drops.

> 1 (12-ounce) package semisweet chocolate morsels
> ¼ cup butter or margarine
> 3½ cups cereal
> ½ cup dried fruit bits

1. Melt the chocolate and butter in a heavy saucepan over medium-low heat, stirring frequently. Or microwave for 2 minutes on HIGH in a large glass bowl; then stir until smooth.

2. Stir in the cereal and dried fruit bits. Drop by heaping teaspoonfuls onto a waxed paper–lined baking sheet. Chill until set.

Yield: about 5 dozen

15-MINUTE RECIPES

■ Mix 1 cup Kellogg's Frosted Rice Krispies with 3 tablespoons melted margarine; press onto the bottom of paper-lined mini-muffin cups. Refrigerate until firm. Fill with lemon curd or hazelnut-chocolate spread. Dollop with whipped topping, if desired.

■ Spread softened strawberry-flavored or plain cream cheese on slices of bread; sprinkle with cinnamon sugar and coarsely crushed Kellogg's Frosted Flakes or General Mills Cinnamon Toast Crunch. Roll the slices tightly, jelly-roll fashion. Brush the outside with melted butter and sprinkle with cinnamon sugar. Bake at 400°F for 10 to 15 minutes, or until toasted.

Easy Chocolate Crispy Bar

Just like a Nestle's Crunch Bar, only better! Any of the "Krispies" will work: Kellogg's Rice Krispies, Cocoa Krispies, or Frosted Rice Krispies.

> 6 ounces chopped semisweet chocolate or semisweet morsels
> 6 ounces chopped white chocolate or morsels
> 1 cup cereal

1. Place the semisweet chocolate and white chocolate in separate glass bowls; microwave each for 1½ to 2 minutes on HIGH; stir until melted.

2. Stir ½ cup of the cereal into each bowl. Alternately spoon the mixtures side by side onto a waxed paper–lined cookie sheet. Swirl together with a knife to marble slightly.

3. Refrigerate for 30 minutes, or until firm enough to break into pieces.

Yield: about ¾ pound

Bran-Nutty Cheese Balls

This is perfect for kids to make for snacks. Nutty bran cereal adds protein; use Kellogg's All-Bran or Bran Buds, Post Grape-Nuts, or Nabisco 100% Bran.

> 1 (3-ounce) package cream cheese
> ½ cup (2 ounces) shredded cheddar or Monterey Jack cheese
> ¼ cup chopped pecans, peanuts, or sunflower seeds
> 1 to 1½ cups coarsely crushed cereal

1. Mash the cream cheese and shredded cheese together in a bowl with a fork; stir in the nuts.

2. Shape into 1-inch balls.

3. Roll in the cereal and refrigerate.

Yield: about 1 dozen

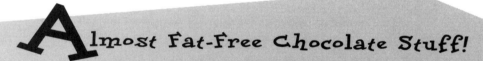

Almost Fat-Free Chocolate Stuff!

These cereal combos taste like your favorite junk food.

Chocolate Peanut Butter Cups: Combine General Mills Reese's Peanut Butter Puffs or Quaker Cap'n Crunch's Peanut Butter Crunch with General Mills Cocoa Puffs.

Nutty Buddy Bar: Add Post Waffle Crisp to the above.

Moon Pies: Combine Quaker Marshmallow Stars or Post Marshmallow Alpha Bits with Kellogg's Cocoa Krispies.

Chocolate Chip Cookies: Mix Ralston Foods Cookie-Crisp with General Mills Cocoa Puffs for extra chocolate taste.

S'mores: Mix Ralston Foods Graham Chex with General Mills Cocoa Puffs and mini marshmallows.

Milky Way: Combine Kellogg's Rice Krispies Treats with Cocoa Krispies.

Quick Peanut Butter and Jelly Oatmeal Crisp Cookies

Because it takes a long time for Quaker Toasted Oatmeal and General Mills Oatmeal Crisp Almond to get soggy in milk, I figured they'd stay crisp in this no-bake cookie. The cookies will not lose their bite if you store them in the refrigerator.

1 (10-ounce) package peanut butter morsels
2 tablespoons butter or margarine
2 tablespoons peanut butter
3½ cups cereal
¼ cup strawberry jelly
1 cup chopped peanuts

1. Combine the peanut butter morsels, butter, and peanut butter in a large saucepan. Cook over medium-low heat, stirring frequently, until melted. Or combine in a large glass bowl and microwave for 1½ to 2 minutes on HIGH; then stir until smooth. Let cool.

2. Stir in the cereal. Drop by tablespoonfuls onto waxed paper and press into 2-inch rounds. Let stand or refrigerate until firm. Stir the jelly until runny; drizzle it on the cookies and sprinkle with peanuts.

Yield: about 3 dozen

Aunt Cora's Special Cookies

This is my earliest memory of a cereal cookie, and my first attempt at cooking. Here is the recipe in my aunt's own words:

Bring to a boil: ½ cup white Karo and ½ cup packed light brown sugar, stirring to melt sugar. Add ½ cup peanut butter. Add 1 cup flaked coconut or chopped pecans and 3 cups Kellogg's Special K. Make into datelike rolls.

—Cora B. Evans

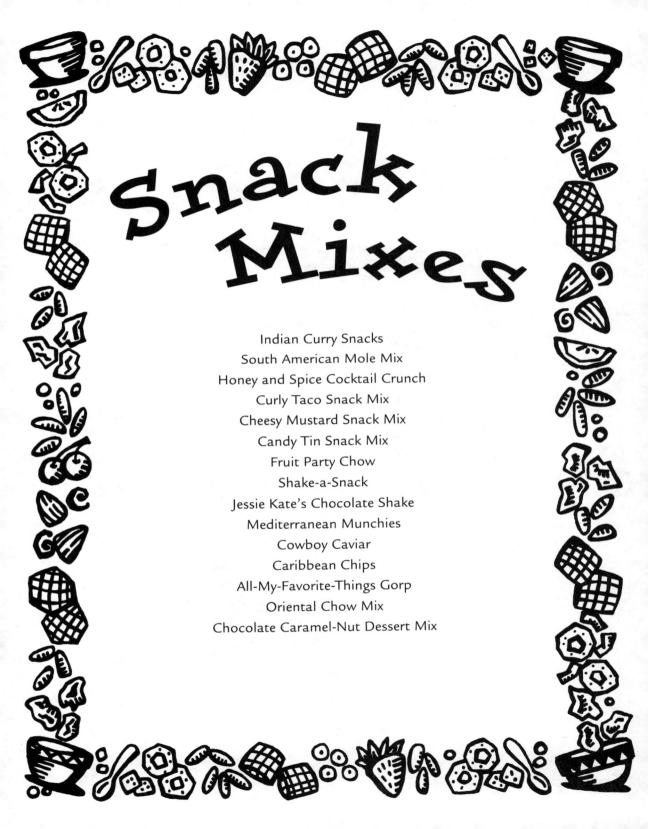

Snack Mixes

Indian Curry Snacks

South American Mole Mix

Honey and Spice Cocktail Crunch

Curly Taco Snack Mix

Cheesy Mustard Snack Mix

Candy Tin Snack Mix

Fruit Party Chow

Shake-a-Snack

Jessie Kate's Chocolate Shake

Mediterranean Munchies

Cowboy Caviar

Caribbean Chips

All-My-Favorite-Things Gorp

Oriental Chow Mix

Chocolate Caramel-Nut Dessert Mix

Indian Curry Snacks

Quaker Toasted Oatmeal Squares, Quaker Oat Bran, Crunchy Corn Bran; Healthy Choice from Kellogg's Multi-Grain Squares; Ralston Foods 100% Whole Grain Wheat Chex, Multi Bran Chex, Rice Chex; or Nabisco Shredded Wheat Spoon Size has a pronounced flavor that is complemented by the spicy sauce mixture.

5 cups cereal

1 cup tiny pretzel twists

1 cup cashews

¼ cup plus 2 tablespoons butter or margarine, melted

1 tablespoon Worcestershire sauce

2½ to 3 teaspoons curry powder

1 teaspoon garlic salt

2 to 3 teaspoons Tabasco or other hot sauce

1 cup unsweetened coconut chips or banana chips

1. Preheat the oven to 300°F.

2. Combine cereal, pretzels, and cashews in a large bowl. Stir together the butter, Worcestershire sauce, curry powder, garlic salt, and Tabasco and drizzle over the cereal mixture, stirring to coat. Spread in an even layer in a large roasting pan or jelly roll pan.

3. Bake for 30 to 40 minutes, stirring every 10 minutes. Let cool; store in an airtight container.

Yield: 8 cups

South American Mole Mix

Use Ralston Foods Corn Chex, Double Chex, Rice Chex, Multi Bran Chex, 100% Whole Grain Wheat Chex; Kellogg's Crispix; Quaker Crunchy Corn Bran; or other cereals that will not get soggy in this sweet-spicy snack mix.

5 cups cereal
3 cups plantain chips
1½ cups dry roasted peanuts
⅓ cup butter or margarine, melted
1 tablespoon chili powder
1 tablespoon Worcestershire sauce
2 teaspoons unsweetened cocoa powder
½ teaspoon garlic salt
½ teaspoon ground cinnamon
¼ to ½ teaspoon cayenne
½ cup raisins

1. Preheat the oven to 250°F.

2. Combine the cereal, plantain chips, and peanuts in a large bowl. Stir together the butter, chili powder, Worcestershire sauce, cocoa powder, garlic salt, cinnamon, and cayenne and drizzle over the cereal mixture, stirring to coat. Spread in an even layer in a large roasting pan or jelly roll pan.

3. Bake for 45 to 50 minutes, stirring every 20 minutes. Let cool; stir in the raisins. Store in an airtight container.

Yield: 10 cups

Honey and Spice Cocktail Crunch

You'll get hooked on this popcorn mix. I use Kellogg's Corn Pops, which tastes like sweet popcorn, but General Mills Cheerios and Kix and Quaker Toasted Oatmeal Squares and Life are great in it, too.

8 cups cereal
4 cups popped popcorn
¼ cup honey
¼ cup light corn syrup
3 tablespoons butter or margarine
3 tablespoons light brown sugar
¼ teaspoon salt
1 teaspoon ground cinnamon
¼ teaspoon baking soda
½ teaspoon vanilla extract
1 cup banana chips
1 cup honey-roasted peanuts or cashews

1. Preheat the oven to 250°F.

2. Combine the cereal and popcorn in a large bowl; set aside.

3. Combine the honey, corn syrup, butter, brown sugar, and salt in a medium saucepan; bring to a boil over medium heat, stirring constantly until the sugar melts. Boil, without stirring, for 7 minutes, or until a candy thermometer registers 250°F.

4. Remove from the heat; stir in the cinnamon, baking soda, and vanilla. Pour over the popcorn-cereal mixture, stirring to coat evenly. Spoon into a greased 15 x 10 x 1-inch jelly roll pan.

5. Bake for 25 minutes, or until golden, stirring every 5 minutes. Stir in the banana chips and nuts. Let cool; store in airtight containers.

Yield: 3 quarts

Curly Taco Snack Mix

These cereals taste great with spicy taco seasoning: Kellogg's Crispix; Ralston Foods Corn Chex, Rice Chex, 100% Whole Grain Wheat Chex, Multi Bran Chex, Double Chex; Nabisco Shredded Wheat Spoon Size; Quaker Crunchy Corn Bran.

> 5 cups cereal
> 2 cups small corn chips or puffed-corn snacks
> 2 cups Cheetos cheese curls
> ⅓ cup butter or margarine, melted
> 1½ to 2 tablespoons commercial taco seasoning mix

1. Preheat the oven to 300°F.

2. Combine the cereal, corn chips, and cheese curls in a large bowl. Stir together the butter and taco seasoning mix and drizzle over the cereal mixture, stirring to coat. Spread in an even layer in a large roasting pan or jelly roll pan.

3. Bake for 30 minutes, stirring every 10 minutes. Let cool; store in an airtight container.

Yield: 8½ cups

Cheesy Mustard Snack Mix

Kellogg's Crispix; Ralston Foods Corn Chex, Rice Chex, 100% Whole Grain Wheat Chex, Multi Bran Chex, Double Chex; and Nabisco Shredded Wheat Spoon Size and Shredded Wheat 'N Bran soak up the butter mixture but will remain crisp after cooking.

5 cups cereal

3 cups broken whole rice cakes or mini rice cakes

1 cup mixed nuts

1 cup tiny pretzel twists

⅓ cup butter or margarine, melted

3 tablespoons Dijon mustard

¾ teaspoon seasoned salt

⅓ cup grated Parmesan cheese

1. Preheat the oven to 300°F.

2. Combine the cereal, rice cakes, nuts, and pretzels in a large bowl. Stir together the butter, mustard, and seasoned salt and drizzle over the cereal mixture, stirring to coat. Spread in an even layer in a large roasting pan or jelly roll pan.

3. Bake for 30 minutes, stirring every 10 minutes. Remove from the oven and stir in the cheese; bake for 5 more minutes. Let cool; store in an airtight container.

Yield: 10 cups

Candy Tin Snack Mix

Make this peanut brittle—like candy cereal mix up to a week ahead and give it away in colorful holiday tins. It's a low-fat candy that your friends will want to get every year. Use a mixture of little nutty, sweet "crunchberries" like Quaker Cap'n Crunch's Deep Sea Crunch, Cap'n Crunch, Popeye Sweet Crunch; Kellogg's Smacks and Corn Pops; or Post Waffle Crisp.

¾ cup light corn syrup
1½ cups sugar
⅛ teaspoon salt
2 (3-inch) cinnamon sticks
1 tablespoon butter or margarine
1½ teaspoons baking soda
4 cups cereal

1. Coat a large baking sheet and a rubber spatula with cooking spray; set aside.

2. Combine the corn syrup, sugar, salt, and cinnamon sticks in a large heavy saucepan; bring to a boil over medium-high heat, stirring constantly. Boil without stirring until the mixture is pale golden brown. Stir in the butter. Cook for 2 to 3 minutes, or until the mixture is amber in color. Remove from the heat; stir in the baking soda. Working quickly, stir in the cereal with the prepared spatula until coated; spread in an even layer on the prepared baking sheet.

3. Let cool for 20 to 30 minutes, or until hardened; break into pieces.

Yield: about 1½ pounds or 24 pieces

Fruity Party Chow

Keep this on hand for an afternoon snack or a lunch-box treat; it even makes a decent breakfast with a glass of milk. Children will love a mixture of any of the following: General Mills Lucky Charms, Frankenberry, Count Chocula, Trix, Berry Berry Kix, Boo Berry, Apple Cinnamon Cheerios, Frosted Cheerios; Kellogg's Froot Loops, Apple Jacks.

4 cups cereal
2 cups teddy bear–shaped graham cookies
1 cup peanuts or milk-chocolate morsels
½ cup raisins or dried fruit bits

1. Combine all of the ingredients in a plastic bag; close and shake to blend.

2. Store in an airtight container in the refrigerator.

Yield: 7½ cups

Shake-a-Snack

No, you don't have to bake these; the oil and dressing mix coat the cereal well. But you do need cereals that will stand up to an oil change, such as: Kellogg's Crispix; Ralston Foods Corn Chex, Rice Chex, 100% Whole Grain Wheat Chex, Multi Bran Chex, Double Chex; General Mills Cheerios; Quaker Crunchy Corn Bran.

4 cups cereal
2 cups small square cheese crackers (Cheese Nips) or small
    round cheese-filled sandwich crackers (Ritz Bits)
2 cups bite-size pretzel nuggets
1 (0.4-ounce) package buttermilk salad dressing mix
3½ tablespoons vegetable or canola oil

1. Combine the cereal, cheese crackers, pretzels, and salad dressing mix in a large plastic bag; close and shake until evenly coated. Pour the oil into the bag, seal, and shake to coat evenly.

2. Store in a sealable plastic bag or an airtight container.

Yield: 8 cups

Jessie Kate's
Chocolate Shake

My daughter made this up to take to school for dessert. It's one of our compromises: healthy cereal and chocolate and marshmallows. Mix the unsweetened cereals that your family likes; squares and round shapes work best because they hold up under the chocolate coating. Here are the cereals Jessie Kate eats in the mix: Ralston Foods Corn Chex, Rice Chex, 100% Whole Grain Wheat Chex, Multi Bran Chex, Graham Chex; General Mills Cheerios or Kix; Quaker Toasted Oatmeal Squares; Post Waffle Crisp.

> 9 cups cereal
> 1½ cups powdered sugar
> 3 cups miniature marshmallows
> 1 cup semisweet chocolate morsels
> ¼ cup stick margarine or butter
> 1 teaspoon vanilla extract
> 1 cup peanuts (optional)

1. Place the cereal in a large bowl; set aside. Place the powdered sugar in a large zip-top plastic bag; set aside.

2. Melt 1 cup of the marshmallows, the chocolate, and margarine in a heavy saucepan. Remove from the heat and stir in vanilla. Pour over the cereal and toss until the pieces are evenly coated.

3. Add the coated cereal to the sugar; seal the bag and shake gently until the pieces are evenly coated. Pour onto a large piece of waxed paper and let cool.

4. Before serving, add the remaining 2 cups marshmallows and the peanuts, if desired, to the cereal mixture. Store in an airtight container.

Yield: 10½ cups

Note: ½-cup peanut butter may be substituted for 1 cup marshmallows in the melted chocolate mixture.

Mediterranean Munchies

Olive oil and balsamic vinegar give these cereals new flavor: Kellogg's Crispix; Ralston Foods Corn Chex, Rice Chex, 100% Whole Grain Wheat Chex, Multi Bran Chex, Double Chex; Nabisco Shredded Wheat Spoon Size, Shredded Wheat 'N Bran.

5 cups cereal

3 cups broken garlic- or sesame-flavored pita chips

1½ cups walnut pieces

½ cup olive oil

3 tablespoons balsamic vinegar

2 teaspoons dried oregano, crushed

1½ teaspoons garlic salt

1 cup slivered dried apricots

1. Preheat the oven to 300°F.

2. Combine the cereal, pita chips, and walnuts in a large bowl. Stir together the olive oil, vinegar, oregano, and garlic salt and drizzle over the cereal mixture, stirring to coat. Spread in an even layer in a large roasting pan or jelly roll pan.

3. Bake for 30 to 40 minutes, stirring every 15 minutes. Let cool; stir in the apricots. Store in an airtight container.

Yield: 11 cups

■ **Italian Munchies:** Prepare as above, substituting dried basil for the oregano and slivered oil-packed sundried tomatoes for the apricots.

Cereal Gets the Bronze

Here are the food industry's three top-selling grocery items, in order: carbonated beverages, milk, and ready-to-eat cereal. Although it may be hard to imagine cooking a gourmet dinner with that shopping list, many folks can and do survive on a refrigerator stocked with cola, milk, and Cheerios.

Cowboy Caviar

*Mexican seasoning contains salt and a chili powder blend. If you can't find it, use
1 tablespoon chili powder, 1 to 1½ teaspoons ground cumin, and ½ teaspoon salt. Fried
pork rind is packaged like potato chips; you can leave it out if it is not distributed in your
area of the country. Use a blend of these cereals: Ralston Foods Corn Chex, Rice Chex,
Double Chex, Multi Bran Chex, 100% Whole Grain Wheat Chex; Kellogg's Crispix.*

> 5 cups cereal
>
> 3 cups broken tortilla chips
>
> 2 cups fried pork rind (optional)
>
> 8 (0.16-ounce) sticks beef jerky, chopped (about ½ cup)
>
> 1 cup peanuts
>
> ¼ cup plus 2 tablespoons butter or margarine, melted
>
> 1½ tablespoons Mexican seasoning
>
> 1 teaspoon Tabasco or other hot sauce

1. Preheat the oven to 300°F.

2. Combine the cereal, tortilla chips, pork rind, if desired, beef jerky, and
   peanuts in a large bowl. Stir together the butter, Mexican seasoning, and
   Tabasco and drizzle over the cereal mixture, stirring to coat. Spread in an
   even layer in a large roasting pan or jelly roll pan.

3. Bake for 30 to 35 minutes, stirring every 10 minutes. Let cool; store in an
   airtight container.

Yield: 9 to 11 cups

Caribbean Chips

This mix will spice up your party. Use any combination of Quaker Toasted Oatmeal Squares; Kellogg's Corn Pops; Ralston Foods Rice Chex, Corn Chex, Double Chex, Multi Bran Chex, Graham Chex; and General Mills Cheerios.

6 cups cereal
2 cups sesame sticks
½ cup shelled sunflower seeds
¼ cup plus 2 tablespoons butter or margarine
¼ cup guava or apple jelly
1½ tablespoons soy sauce
¼ teaspoon seasoned salt
½ teaspoon cayenne
1 cup banana chips
1 cup finely chopped candied pineapple or dried fruit bits

1. Preheat the oven to 250°F.

2. Combine the cereal, sesame sticks, and sunflower seeds in a large bowl.

3. Combine the butter, jelly, soy sauce, seasoned salt, and cayenne in a small saucepan; cook over medium heat, stirring constantly, until the butter melts. Drizzle over the cereal mixture, stirring to coat.

4. Spread in an even layer in a large roasting pan or jelly roll pan. Bake at 250°F for 45 to 50 minutes, or until golden brown, stirring every 15 minutes. Let cool; stir in the banana chips and candied pineapple. Store in an airtight container.

Yield: 13 cups

All-My-Favorite-Things Gorp

Take this stuff on a hike, or pack it in a dry-bag in your kayak. I keep a large jar of it in the refrigerator, because I never know when the itch for a road trip will strike, or when my daughter just needs a bag of something to eat on her way to soccer practice. The jar gets constantly fed with ends of cereal boxes that may have only one bowl left, as well as the dregs of packages of candies, nuts, pretzels, and other munchies. Here's the basic formula to mix as a gorp starter; you'll end up with all your favorite cereals mixed in if you keep it "growing." By the way, my personal favorite cereal to use is Quaker Toasted Oatmeal Squares; I feel as if I'm eating a thick, sweet English tea biscuit-cracker and not a cereal square. Add General Mills Golden Grahams, and I'm in carbo-loaded heaven. Also good: General Mills Cheerios or Honey Nut Cheerios; Ralston Foods Rice Chex, Corn Chex, Double Chex, 100% Whole Grain Wheat Chex, Multi Bran Chex, Graham Chex; Kellogg's Crispix.

8 cups cereal

2 cups semisweet chocolate mini morsels

1 cup dried coconut flakes

1 cup sunflower seeds

1 cup dry-roasted peanuts or shelled pistachios

1 cup raisins

1 cup chopped candied pineapple

1. Combine all ingredients in a large bowl.

2. Store in an airtight container.

Yield: 15 cups

Oriental Chow Mix

Nabisco Shredded Wheat Spoon Size and Shredded Wheat 'N Bran taste especially good in this Oriental sauce mixture. Add Ralston Foods Rice Chex, Corn Chex, 100% Whole Grain Wheat Chex, Multi Bran Chex, Double Chex; Kellogg's Crispix; or Quaker Crunchy Corn Bran for variety.

5 cups cereal

2 cups chow mein noodles

2 cups Oriental rice snacks or broken rice crackers

1 cup soy nuts or peanuts

¼ cup plus 2 tablespoons butter or margarine, melted

3 tablespoons teriyaki sauce

1½ teaspoons ground ginger

2 to 3 teaspoons dark sesame oil

½ teaspoon salt

½ teaspoon cayenne

1. Preheat the oven to 250°F.

2. Combine the cereal, chow mein noodles, rice snacks, and soy nuts in a large bowl. Stir together the butter, teriyaki sauce, ginger, oil, salt, and cayenne and drizzle over the cereal mixture, stirring to coat. Spread in an even layer in a large roasting pan or jelly roll pan.

3. Bake for 40 to 45 minutes, stirring every 20 minutes. Let cool; store in an airtight container.

Yield: 9 cups

Chocolate Caramel-Nut Dessert Mix

This tastes like almond bark but with crunchy things. Use unsweetened cereals such as: Ralston Foods Rice Chex, Corn Chex, Double Chex; Kellogg's Crispix; General Mills Cheerios.

16 cups cereal

8 cups tiny pretzels

3 cups sugar

½ cup light corn syrup

½ cup dark corn syrup

⅔ cup water

¼ cup plus 2 tablespoons butter or margarine

½ teaspoon salt

½ teaspoon baking soda

2 teaspoons vanilla extract

1 (12-ounce) package semisweet chocolate morsels

1 cup chopped peanuts or toasted sliced almonds

1. Spread the cereal and pretzels in 2 large, deep roasting pans.

2. Bring the sugar, corn syrups, and water to a boil in a large saucepan. Add the butter and cook, stirring occasionally, until a candy thermometer registers 300° to 310°F (or until the mixture forms a hard thread when dropped into cold water). Remove from the heat; carefully stir in the salt, baking soda, and vanilla with a long-handled wooden spoon (the mixture will spatter and foam). Pour immediately over the cereal mixture and stir quickly to coat. Spread in even layers in the roasting pans; let cool.

3. Break up large chunks of the mixture and spread on 2 large baking sheets. Place the chocolate in a glass bowl; microwave for two minutes on HIGH and stir until smooth (or melt in a saucepan over medium-low heat). Drizzle over the cereal mixture and sprinkle immediately with the nuts. Let stand at room temperature until the chocolate hardens. Store in an airtight container.

Yield: 2½ pounds

Bars and Cookies

Bars

Magic Chocolate Cereal Bars

Pucker Up Lemon Squares

Caramel Graham Squares

Nutty Buddies

Gooey Butterscotch Cereal Bars

White Chocolate Almond Bars

Cranberry Whole-Grain Nut Bars

Honey-Roasted Pecan Fudge Bars

Chocolate Nougat Crispy Bars

Granola Biker Bars

Granola Blondies

Quick Raisin and Nut Energy Bars

Apple Date Crunch Bars

Rocky Road Clusters Fudge

Cookies

White Chocolate Macaroons

Granola Wedding Cookies

Design Your Own Monster Cookies

Double Chocolate Chip Cookie Chocolate Chip Cookies

Frosted Almond Raisin Carrot Cookies

Vanilla Nut Biscotti

BARS

Magic Chocolate Cereal Bars

You may have had an original version of these at a bakery or coffee shop, or even made them at home. This one uses two of my favorite cereals in one recipe, which makes it magic as far as I'm concerned. Use Ralston Foods Graham Chex or General Mills Golden Grahams in the crust and fruitless granola for the top: Kellogg's Low Fat Granola without Raisins, Quaker Sun Country Granola with Almonds, or Quaker 100% Natural Granola Oats & Honey.

½ cup butter or margarine

3 cups crushed cereal

1 (14-ounce) can low-fat sweetened condensed milk

1 cup semisweet chocolate morsels or M&M baking bits

½ cup flaked coconut

½ cup pecans

2½ cups granola

1. Preheat the oven to 350°F.

2. Place the butter in a 13 x 9 x 2-inch baking pan; place in the oven until the butter melts.

3. Sprinkle the cereal crumbs evenly over the butter; stir well and spread in an even layer. Pour the sweetened condensed milk evenly over the crumbs. Sprinkle with the chocolate, coconut, nuts, and granola; press down firmly.

4. Bake for 25 to 30 minutes, or until lightly browned. Cool completely; chill if desired. Cut into bars.

Yield: 3 dozen

Pucker Up Lemon Squares

Lemon custard tops a yummy cereal crust. Serve these for dessert with fresh berries or eat them with a big glass of milk or iced tea for a snack. (I eat them for breakfast because I have no willpower. And, after all, they do contain cereal and eggs.) Use General Mills Kix; Kellogg's Rice Krispies; even Post Waffle Crisp.

1½ cups finely crushed cereal

½ cup plus 3 tablespoons all-purpose flour

⅓ cup powdered sugar plus additional for sprinkling

½ cup butter or margarine, softened

4 large eggs

1 cup sugar

2 teaspoons freshly grated lemon rind

¼ cup plus 2 tablespoons lemon juice

½ teaspoon baking powder

1. Preheat the oven to 350°F.

2. Combine the cereal, ½ cup of the flour, and ⅓ cup powdered sugar in a medium bowl; cut in the butter using a pastry blender or a fork until well blended. Press firmly into the bottom of an ungreased 8-inch square baking pan; bake for 10 to 12 minutes, or until lightly browned.

3. Combine the eggs, sugar, lemon rind, lemon juice, the remaining 3 tablespoons flour, and the baking powder in a medium mixing bowl. Beat until blended. Pour over the hot crust.

4. Bake for 15 minutes, or until the center is set. Cool in the pan on a wire rack. Sprinkle with powdered sugar; cut into squares.

Yield: 16 squares

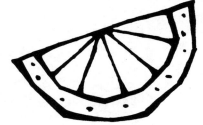

Caramel Graham Squares

You won't believe the wonderfully goopy topping the ice-cream topping sauce makes on these bars. To get great graham taste in the crust, use General Mills Golden Grahams or S'Mores Grahams; or Ralston Foods Graham Chex.

2½ cups coarsely crushed cereal

2⅓ cups all-purpose flour

½ cup firmly packed light brown sugar

1 teaspoon baking soda

¼ teaspoon salt

1 cup butter or margarine, melted

1 (12-ounce) package semisweet chocolate morsels

1 cup chopped pecans or peanuts

1 (12.25-ounce) jar caramel ice-cream topping

1. Preheat the oven to 350°F.

2. Combine the cereal, 2 cups of the flour, the brown sugar, baking soda, and salt in a large bowl. Stir in the butter until blended. Measure out and reserve 1½ cups (for topping); press the remaining mixture into an ungreased 13 x 9 x 2-inch baking pan. Bake for 15 minutes, or until lightly browned.

3. Sprinkle with the chocolate and nuts. Combine the ice-cream topping and the remaining ⅓ cup flour, mixing well; drizzle over the cookie crust. Sprinkle with the reserved cereal/flour mixture.

4. Bake for 20 to 25 minutes, or until lightly browned. Cool in the pan on a wire rack; cut into squares.

Yield: 2½ dozen

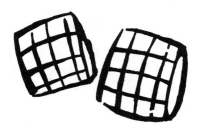

Nutty Buddies

Those peanut butter wafer cookie candy bars dipped in chocolate are my all-time favorite junk food. I've tried to duplicate them many times, but I didn't get it right until I wrote this cereal book. General Mills Kix or Kellogg's Corn Pops gives the best wafer cookie texture. The candy coating, also called candy-making almond bark, comes in white chocolate as well as regular chocolate flavors.

½ cup butter or margarine
1¾ cups smooth peanut butter
1⅔ cups powdered sugar
2 cups crushed cereal
24 ounces chocolate-flavored candy coating, chopped

1. Combine the butter and peanut butter in a saucepan; cook over medium heat, stirring constantly, until melted. Let cool to room temperature.

2. Combine the powdered sugar and cereal in a large bowl; pour in the butter mixture and mix well. Press into a foil-lined and greased 9-inch square baking pan. Place a piece of plastic wrap over the mixture and press down firmly to compact it. Cover and refrigerate until well chilled.

3. Lift out the foil and place it on a cutting board. Cut into bars. Melt the candy coating in a large saucepan over medium-low heat, stirring frequently; dip the bars in the coating. Place the bars on a wire rack and refrigerate until the coating hardens. Store in the refrigerator.

Yield: 32 bars

Note: Two 12-ounce packages of semisweet chocolate morsels may be substituted for the candy coating.

Gooey Butterscotch Cereal Bars

Here's another layered bar that is simple to make. General Mills Golden Grahams as well as Ralston Foods Graham Chex, Rice Chex, or Multi Bran Chex stay extra crispy on top.

> 6 cups cereal
> ⅔ cup butter or margarine
> 1½ cups butterscotch or peanut butter morsels
> 1½ cups flaked coconut
> 1 (14-ounce) can low-fat or regular sweetened condensed milk
> 1 cup honey-roasted or plain pecans or peanuts

1. Preheat the oven to 350°F.

2. Coarsely crush 4 cups of the cereal. Place the butter in a 13 x 9 x 2-inch baking pan and bake until the butter melts. Sprinkle the crushed cereal over the butter; toss and spread in an even layer. Top evenly with the butterscotch, coconut, condensed milk, nuts, and the remaining 2 cups cereal. Press down firmly.

3. Bake for 25 to 30 minutes, or until lightly browned. Cool completely in the pan on a wire rack. Cut into bars.

Yield: 3 dozen

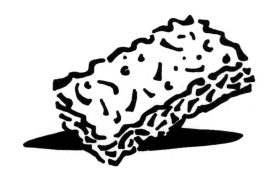

White Chocolate Almond Bars

So simple you could make them in your sleep, but the taste is out of this world. Most of the indulgence comes from the dessert-tasting cereal ingredients: Ralston Foods Almond Delight or Kellogg's Temptations French Vanilla Almond.

3½ cups cereal

⅓ cup apricot or ginger preserves

¼ cup plus 2 tablespoons butter or margarine

6 (1-ounce) squares white chocolate, chopped

1. Place the cereal in a large bowl. Melt the preserves, butter, and 4 ounces of the white chocolate in a small saucepan. Pour over the cereal and mix well.

2. Scrape the mixture into a greased 8-inch square baking pan; cover with plastic wrap. Place another 8-inch square baking pan or a heavy book on top; press to compact the mixture into a firm, even layer. Refrigerate for 30 minutes, or until cool.

3. Place the remaining 2 ounces white chocolate in a small glass bowl; microwave for 30 to 45 seconds on HIGH; stir until smooth. Drizzle over the bars. Refrigerate for 1 hour, or until firm. Cut into bars.

Yield: 25 bars

Cranberry Whole-Grain Nut Bars

You'll want to make this your signature bar: perfect to wrap for presents or exchange in cookie swaps. You can make them up to a month ahead of time. Just transfer the bars to plastic freezer bags, seal, and freeze. The following cereals will contribute slightly different flavors but the same texture, so let your taste buds be your guide: Post Great Grains Crunchy Pecan; Ralston Foods Cranberry Walnut or Blueberry Pecan Muesli.

> 2 cups cereal
> ½ cups all-purpose flour
> ¾ cup firmly packed light brown sugar
> ½ teaspoon baking soda
> ⅔ cup butter or margarine, melted
> 1 (16-ounce) can whole-berry cranberry sauce

1. Preheat the oven to 350°F.

2. Combine the cereal, flour, brown sugar, and baking soda in a large bowl; stir in the butter. Press two-thirds of the mixture into the bottom of a greased 9-inch square baking pan.

3. Bake for 12 to 14 minutes, or until lightly browned.

4. Gently spread the cranberry sauce over the crust. Sprinkle with the reserved cereal-flour mixture, pressing it lightly into the cranberry sauce. Bake for 25 to 30 additional minutes, or until golden. Cool in the pan on a wire rack. Cut into bars.

Yield: 25 bars

Honey-Roasted Pecan Fudge Bars

This is the most incredibly indulgent bar ever. But you'll have to save enough Kellogg's Temptations Honey Roasted Pecan cereal for the bars after you eat it straight out of the box.

1 cup plus 2 tablespoons butter or margarine, softened
2 cups sugar
2½ cups all-purpose flour
2 large eggs
1 tablespoon plus 1 teaspoon vanilla extract
1 teaspoon baking soda
3⅓ cups cereal
1 (14-ounce) can sweetened condensed milk
1½ cups semisweet chocolate morsels
½ cup chopped pecans, toasted

1. Preheat the oven to 350°F.

2. Cream 1 cup of the butter and the sugar in a large mixing bowl with an electric mixer at medium speed. Add 1¼ cups of the flour, the eggs, 2 teaspoons of the vanilla, and the baking soda, beating at low speed until blended. Beat in the remaining 1¼ cups flour and stir in the cereal. Press two-thirds of the mixture into the bottom of an ungreased 15 x 10 x 1-inch jelly roll pan. Set aside. Reserve the remaining mixture for crumb topping.

3. Combine the condensed milk, chocolate, and the remaining 2 tablespoons butter in a saucepan. Cook over medium-low heat until the chocolate melts, stirring occasionally. Remove from the heat; stir in the remaining 2 teaspoons vanilla and the pecans. Pour over the crust and dot with the reserved crumb mixture.

4. Bake for 25 minutes, or until the top is lightly golden. Let cool in the pan on a wire rack. Cut into bars.

Yield: 60 bars

Chocolate Nougat Crispy Bars

Extra rich and chewy, these taste just like a candy bar. To get the "crispy" in these bars, you have to use them: Kellogg's Cocoa Krispies, Rice Krispies, or Frosted Rice Krispies.

1 (11½-ounce) package milk-chocolate morsels
½ cup butterscotch or peanut butter morsels
½ cup creamy peanut butter
3 cups cereal
1 cup sugar
¼ cup milk
¼ cup butter or margarine
¼ cup marshmallow creme
1 teaspoon vanilla extract
2 cups unsalted roasted peanuts
1 (14-ounce) package caramels, unwrapped
2 tablespoons hot water

1. Melt the chocolate, butterscotch, and peanut butter in a large heavy saucepan over medium heat. Remove from the heat; measure out half of the mixture and reserve. Stir the cereal into the remaining mixture; spread in a greased 13 x 9 x 2-inch baking pan.

2. Bring the sugar, milk, and butter to a boil in a heavy saucepan, stirring constantly until the sugar melts. Boil, without stirring, for 5 minutes. Stir in the marshmallow creme and vanilla. Pour over the cereal layer and sprinkle with the peanuts.

3. Melt the caramels and water in a heavy saucepan over medium heat. Drizzle over the peanuts.

4. Spread the reserved chocolate mixture evenly over the caramel layer. Cool completely, and cut into bars.

Yield: 2 dozen

Granola Biker Bars

Packaged granola bars have nothing on these. Use any of the following granolas: C. W. Post Hearty Granola; Quaker Sun Country Granola—Raisin and Date, 100% Natural Low Fat Granola with Raisins, 100% Natural Oats, Honey, & Raisins, 100% Natural Granola Oats & Honey; General Mills Nature Valley Low Fat Fruit Granola; Kellogg's Low Fat Granola with Raisins. Stored in an airtight container, these bars will stay moist and soft for 4 or 5 days.

1 cup firmly packed light brown sugar

¼ cup butter or margarine, softened

¼ cup honey

2 egg whites, lightly beaten

1 cup all-purpose flour

1 teaspoon ground cinnamon

½ teaspoon baking powder

3 cups cereal

1 cup raisins or semisweet chocolate mini morsels

½ cup shelled sunflower seeds or chopped peanuts

1. Preheat the oven to 350°F.

2. Combine the brown sugar, butter, honey, and egg whites in a large bowl; beat with an electric mixer at medium speed until well blended. Beat in the flour, cinnamon, and baking powder. Stir in the cereal, raisins, and sunflower seeds.

3. Press the mixture firmly into a greased 13 x 9 x 2-inch baking pan; bake for 20 minutes, or until the edges are lightly browned and the center appears set. Let cool completely in the pan on a wire rack. Cut into bars.

Yield: 30 bars

Granola Blondies

For the blonde brownie lover, this decadent version trades nuts for Kellogg's Low Fat Granola without Raisins; Quaker Sun Country Granola with Almonds, 100% Natural Granola Oats & Honey.

½ cup butter or margarine, melted
½ cup firmly packed light brown sugar
⅓ cup sugar
2 large eggs
1 teaspoon vanilla extract
½ teaspoon baking soda
½ teaspoon salt
1 cup all-purpose flour
2 cups cereal

1. Preheat the oven to 350°F.

2. Whisk together the butter and sugars in a large bowl. Add the eggs, vanilla, baking soda, and salt; whisk until smooth. Stir in the flour and cereal.

3. Scrape the batter into a foil-lined and greased 8- or 9-inch baking pan. Bake for 25 to 35 minutes, or until a wooden toothpick inserted in the center comes out almost clean. Let cool in the pan on a wire rack. Lift the foil out of the pan and cut into bars.

Yield: 20 bars

Quick Raisin and Nut Energy Bars

Take these to the gym for a boost. For maximum texture, use: General Mills Raisin Nut Bran; Kellogg's Just Right with Crunchy Nuggets, Nutri-Grain Almond Raisin, Mueslix Crispy Blend; Post Great Grains Crunchy Pecan or Great Grains Raisin, Date, Pecan.

¾ cup firmly packed light brown sugar
⅔ cup honey
1 cup peanut butter
6 cups cereal
½ cup dried fruit bits

1. Bring the brown sugar and honey to a boil in a heavy saucepan, stirring until the sugar melts. Remove from the heat and stir in the peanut butter until smooth.

2. Place the cereal and fruit bits in a large bowl. Pour the sugar mixture over the cereal mixture and toss well to coat. Spread into a greased 13 x 9 x 2-inch baking pan; place a piece of plastic wrap on top and press firmly to compact. Let cool. Remove plastic wrap and cut into bars; wrap individually in plastic wrap, if desired.

Yield: 2 dozen

Apple Date Crunch Bars

Good, and good for you. Hand these out for after-school snacks, breakfast-on-the-run, and lunch-box treats. For the best apple flavor, use Kellogg's Mueslix Crispy Blend Apple & Almond Crunch.

1 cup firmly packed light brown sugar
¾ cup apple juice
1½ cups finely diced peeled apples
1 cup chopped dates
1¾ cups all-purpose flour
½ teaspoon baking soda
¼ teaspoon salt
¾ cup butter or margarine
2 cups cereal

1. Preheat the oven to 375°F.

2. Combine ¾ cup of the brown sugar, the apple juice, apples, and dates in a large heavy saucepan; bring to a boil. Reduce the heat and simmer for 10 minutes, or until thickened, stirring occasionally. Let cool and set aside.

3. Combine the flour, the remaining ¼ cup brown sugar, the baking soda, and salt in a large bowl. Cut in the butter with a fork or pastry blender until the mixture is crumbly. Mix in the cereal. Evenly press 3 cups of the mixture into a greased and floured 9-inch square baking pan. Spread the cooled apple mixture evenly on top. Sprinkle with the remaining cereal mixture and press down lightly.

4. Bake for 20 to 25 minutes, or until golden brown. Let cool completely in the pan; cut into bars.

Yield: 20 bars

Rocky Road Clusters Fudge

If you don't have time to wait, drop this quick mixture by spoonfuls onto a plate and freeze until solid. General Mills Raisin Nut Bran or Clusters; Post Honey Bunches of Oats; or Quaker Toasted Oatmeal with Almonds adds just the right crunch.

> 1 (14-ounce) can fat-free, low-fat, or regular sweetened condensed milk
> 1 (12-ounce) package semisweet chocolate morsels
> 2 tablespoons butter or margarine
> 6 cups cereal
> 1 cup miniature marshmallows

1. Combine the condensed milk, chocolate, and butter in a heavy saucepan; cook over medium heat until the chocolate melts, stirring constantly. Or combine in a glass bowl; microwave for 2 to 3 minutes on HIGH and stir until smooth.

2. Pour over the cereal in a large bowl and stir until almost coated. Add the marshmallows and stir until well coated. Press into a greased or plastic wrap–lined 13 x 9 x 2-inch baking pan. Cover with plastic wrap, pressing down to compact the mixture. Refrigerate until cold; cut into bars. Store in the refrigerator.

Yield: about 4 dozen

COOKIES

White Chocolate Macaroons

*Kellogg's Temptations French Vanilla Almond or General Mills Oatmeal Crisp Almond
has lots of nuts and the perfect sugar-coated flake to add unique texture to these coconut
confections. White chocolate morsels make them, in my opinion, perfect.*

¼ cup butter or margarine, softened

1 (3-ounce) package cream cheese, softened

⅔ cup sugar

1 large egg

1 teaspoon vanilla extract

1 teaspoon almond extract

1 cup all-purpose flour

1 teaspoon baking powder

¼ teaspoon salt

2 cups cereal, crushed

1 cup flaked coconut

1 (11-ounce) package white baking morsels

1. Preheat the oven to 275°F.

2. Beat the butter, cream cheese, and sugar in a large mixing bowl with an
   electric mixer until light and fluffy. Add the egg, vanilla, and almond, beating
   well. Combine the flour, baking powder, and salt; add to the creamed
   mixture, mixing well. Stir in the cereal, coconut, and baking morsels.

3. Drop the mixture by tablespoonfuls onto greased baking sheets. Bake for
   30 minutes, or until light golden brown. Let cool for 5 minutes on the baking
   sheets; transfer to wire racks and let cool completely.

Yield: 3½ dozen

Granola Wedding Cookies

These delicate, buttery cookies are typically made with finely chopped nuts and rolled in powdered sugar. You can duplicate the nutty texture by crushing one of these granolas without fruit: Quaker Sun Country Granola with Almonds, 100% Natural Granola Oats & Honey; Kellogg's Low Fat Granola without Raisins. (If you use a granola with fruit, it will be gooey when crushed.)

¾ cup unsalted butter, softened
¾ cup powdered sugar plus additional for rolling
½ teaspoon salt
1 tablespoon milk
2 teaspoons vanilla extract
1¾ cups all-purpose flour
1½ cups cereal, crushed

1. Preheat the oven to 300°F.

2. Beat the butter in a large mixing bowl with an electric mixer until light and fluffy. Add the powdered sugar, salt, milk, and vanilla; beat at medium speed until blended. Stir in the flour until a soft dough forms. Stir in the cereal until well mixed. Cover and refrigerate for 4 hours or overnight.

3. Remove the dough from the refrigerator 15 minutes before forming the cookies. Shape the dough with your hands by ½ tablespoonfuls into small, 2 x ½-inch fingers or balls. Place about ½ inch apart on a large, lightly greased baking sheet. Bake for 30 to 40 minutes, or until the bottoms of the cookies are golden but the tops are still pale. Roll the warm cookies in powdered sugar; cool on a rack. Roll again in powdered sugar when cool, and store in an airtight container.

Yield: about 56 cookies

Design Your Own Monster Cookies

Monstrously good—and huge—these cookies contain wonderful things that set them apart from all others: cereal, peanut butter, and M&Ms. You could also cut your favorite chocolate bar into small pieces and use it in place of the M&Ms and/or morsels. Cereal makes the cookies chewy, yet crisp. Choose from: Quaker Toasted Oatmeal Cereal (Honey Nut or Original); Post Honey Bunches of Oats; General Mills Oatmeal Crisp Almond; Kellogg's Nut & Honey Crunch.

1 cup all-purpose flour

2 teaspoons baking soda

½ teaspoon salt

½ cup butter or margarine, softened

1 cup sugar

1 cup firmly packed light brown sugar

3 large eggs

2 cups peanut butter (creamy or crunchy)

2 teaspoons vanilla extract

4 cups cereal

1 cup M&Ms baking pieces or coarsely chopped peanuts

1 cup semisweet chocolate, milk-chocolate, peanut butter, or butterscotch morsels

1. Preheat the oven to 350°F.

2. Combine the flour, baking soda, and salt; mix well.

3. Cream the butter and sugars until fluffy in a large mixing bowl. Add the eggs one at a time, beating well after each addition. Beat in the peanut butter and vanilla. Gradually beat in the flour mixture at low speed until blended. Stir in the cereal, M&Ms, and chocolate by hand: the dough will be stiff.

4. For each cookie, pack the dough into a ¼-cup measure. Drop onto lightly greased baking sheets, spacing 4 inches apart. Lightly press each cookie into a 3-inch circle. Bake for 12 to 14 minutes, or until lightly browned; the centers of the cookies will be slightly soft. Cool for 5 minutes on baking sheets; transfer to wire racks and cool completely.

Yield: 3 dozen

Just How Much Cereal Do We Eat?

Even as you read this, cereal wars rage and prices are coming down. Thankfully, that may change the following numbers from the Nielsen Consumer Information Services by encouraging us to pick up *lots* of boxes: some to bake these cookies with and some just to eat.

Until then, here are current statistics, and they haven't changed much over the past 5 years:

Shoppers spend an average of $74.55 per household per year on cereal. The big spenders are families with children aged 6 to 17, who eat $122 worth of flakes, Os, shreds, and the good stuff. Singles will spend less than the national average, which makes sense because there is only one person eating it. However, when you figure that they spend an average of $35 *by themselves* and if you multiply that by two in case they live with someone else, you'll get close enough to that first average. The point is, we all are eating a lot of cereal.

Double Chocolate Chip Cookie Chocolate Chip Cookies

How can you beat a chocolate chip cookie with chocolate chip cookie cereal in it? Ralston Foods Cookie-Crisp Cereal makes the cookie taste like an even better chocolate chip cookie—or does the recipe make the cereal taste more like a chocolate chip cookie? Anyway, these are terrific for breakfast, with a cup of coffee for dunking. If you love oats in your cookies, they are extra yummy with Quaker Toasted Oatmeal, and just as chocolaty.

½ cup butter or margarine, softened
½ cup firmly packed light brown sugar
¼ cup sugar
1 large egg
1 teaspoon vanilla extract
1¼ cups all-purpose flour
½ teaspoon baking soda
¼ teaspoon salt
6 ounces (1 cup) semisweet chocolate morsels
2 cups cereal

1. Preheat the oven to 375°F.

2. Cream the butter and sugars in a large mixing bowl until fluffy. Add the egg and vanilla, blending well.

3. Combine the flour, baking soda, and salt; add the flour mixture to the creamed mixture, stirring just until blended. Stir in the chocolate and cereal.

4. Drop the dough by rounded tablespoonfuls 2 inches apart onto lightly greased baking sheets. Flatten the cookies slightly; bake for 13 to 15 minutes, or until lightly browned. Transfer to a wire rack and cool completely.

Yield: about 26 cookies

Frosted Almond Raisin Carrot Cookies

Do you like carrot cake or carrot-nut muffins? For the same great taste in a smaller bite, try one of these cereals: Kellogg's Mueslix Raisin & Almond Crunch with Dates, Just Right Fruit & Nut, Nutri-Grain Almond Raisin; General Mills Basic 4; Post Fruit & Fibre Dates, Raisins, Walnuts or Great Grains Raisin, Date, Pecan.

1⅔ cups all-purpose flour
1 teaspoon baking powder
¼ teaspoon salt
½ cup butter or margarine, softened
¾ cup sugar
1 large egg
1 teaspoon vanilla extract
2 cups cereal
1 cup finely shredded carrots
2 cups powdered sugar
2 to 3 tablespoons orange juice

1. Preheat the oven to 350°F.

2. Combine the flour, baking powder, and salt; set aside. Cream the butter and sugar in a large mixing bowl until fluffy. Add the egg and vanilla; beat well. Gradually beat in the flour mixture until blended. Stir in the cereal and carrots.

3. Drop the dough by heaping teaspoonfuls 2 inches apart onto ungreased baking sheets. Bake for 12 to 15 minutes, or until the edges are lightly browned. Transfer to wire racks and cool completely.

4. To make the icing, mix the powdered sugar with enough orange juice to make the desired spreading consistency. Spread on the cooled cookies.

Yield: 5 dozen

New Cereals We'd Love to See

I wag my finger at cereal companies for not having thought of the following:

- Trail Mix Cereal: Yogurt-coated Rice Chex or Corn Pops, candy-coated raisins and peanuts, and M&Ms
- Chocolate-Covered or Strawberry-Frosted Donut Cereal
- White Chocolate Cocoa Puffs
- Chocolate Ganache Frosted Flakes
- Snickers Cereal: Caramel-, then chocolate-coated Chex mixed with toffee morsels and peanuts
- Heath Bar Cereal: Toffee candy-coated chocolate Chex or Cocoa Puffs
- Oreo Cookie Cereal: Bite-size cream-filled chocolate wafer cookies
- Ginger Snap Cereal: Frosted rounds of mini gingersnap cookies
- Girl Scout Cookie Cereal: Bite-size Thin Mint cookies or Trefoil butter cookies

Vanilla Nut Biscotti

Serve these with coffee for breakfast or dessert. They're better for you than pastries, and they'll keep in an airtight container for a month. General Mills Honey Nut Cheerios; Kellogg's Nut & Honey Crunch O's; Post Honeycomb; or Quaker OH's—Honey Graham adds ground nut texture to the dough.

> 3 cups cereal, crushed
> 1½ cups Bisquick
> 2 teaspoons ground cinnamon
> ½ cup honey
> 2 large eggs, lightly beaten
> 1 teaspoon vanilla extract
> 1¼ cups toasted slivered almonds, or toasted
>   whole shelled hazelnuts

1. Preheat the oven to 325°F.

2. Combine the cereal, Bisquick, and cinnamon in a large bowl; stir well. Beat together the honey, eggs, and vanilla; add to the cereal mixture and stir well. The mixture will be sticky. Stir in the nuts.

3. Divide the dough into 2 equal portions. On a heavily floured surface, shape each portion into a log about 15 inches long by 2 inches wide. Place the logs 2 inches apart on greased and floured baking sheets. Bake for 30 to 35 minutes, or until firm and golden brown on the bottom. Transfer to a wire rack and cool completely. Reduce oven temperature to 300°F.

4. Using a serrated knife, cut each log into ¾-inch-thick diagonal slices. Place the slices in a single layer on a baking sheet; bake for 15 minutes, or until the tops are golden brown. Turn the slices over and bake for 15 minutes more, or until the biscotti are very dry. Cool on a wire rack.

Yield: 3½ dozen

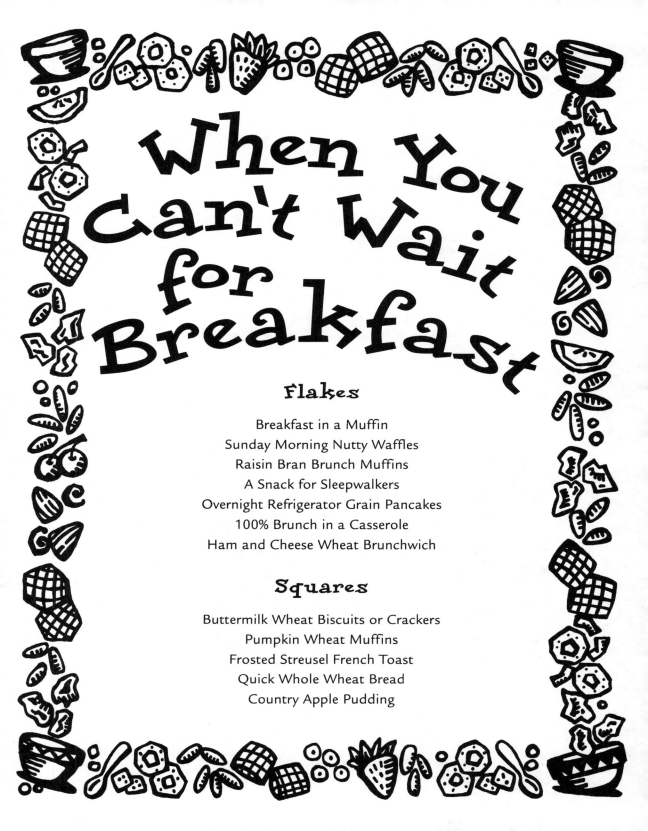

When You Can't Wait for Breakfast

Flakes

Breakfast in a Muffin

Sunday Morning Nutty Waffles

Raisin Bran Brunch Muffins

A Snack for Sleepwalkers

Overnight Refrigerator Grain Pancakes

100% Brunch in a Casserole

Ham and Cheese Wheat Brunchwich

Squares

Buttermilk Wheat Biscuits or Crackers

Pumpkin Wheat Muffins

Frosted Streusel French Toast

Quick Whole Wheat Bread

Country Apple Pudding

Shreds

Lemon Shredded Coffee Cake
Tuscan Shredded Wheat Bread
Frosted Wheat Pastry Twists

The Good Stuff

Hawaiian Banana Banana Bread
Carrot Cake Temptation Muffins and Cupcakes
Chocolate Chip Banana Crunch Muffins
Double Blueberry Morning Muffins
Bran Gingerbread
Lemon Blueberry Bran Bread
The Complete Breakfast Pizza
Hearty Bran Nut Bread
Red, White, and Blue Granola Parfait

"All of These Things Are Very Important If You Are a Connoisseur of Cold Cereal"

"I absolutely never add anything to the cereal like bananas or fruit and I despise any cereal that gets mushy. I also despise people who call me on the phone just after I have added milk to my cereal, which causes it to become mushy while I answer the phone." —**Charles M. Schulz (creator of "Peanuts")**

FLAKES

Breakfast in a Muffin

You can't beat these muffins for breakfast-on-the-run or a mid-morning snack. Warm them in the microwave on MEDIUM, wrapped in a paper towel, for 20 to 30 seconds. Use General Mills Wheaties, Whole Grain Total; Kellogg's Special K, Complete Bran Flakes, Common Sense Oat Bran; Post Bran Flakes.

> 1 large egg, lightly beaten
> 1 cup milk
> ¼ cup vegetable oil
> 1 teaspoon mustard
> ¼ to ½ teaspoon Tabasco or other hot sauce
> 1 cup cereal
> 1¾ cups all-purpose flour
> 2 teaspoons baking powder
> ¼ teaspoon salt
> 1 cup (4 ounces) shredded cheddar or Swiss cheese
> ½ cup finely chopped cooked ham

1. Preheat the oven to 400°F.

2. Combine the egg, milk, oil, mustard, and hot sauce in a large bowl; mix in the cereal. Let stand for 10 minutes.

3. Combine the flour, baking powder, and salt. Add the flour mixture, cheese, and ham to the cereal mixture. Stir until the dry ingredients are just moistened.

4. Spoon into greased muffin pans; bake for 22 to 25 minutes, or until lightly browned. Remove from the pans immediately. Serve hot or at room temperature.

Yield: 1 dozen

Sunday Morning Nutty Waffles

This breakfast will get you ready for a tennis match, a marathon, an afternoon of golf, or whatever sport gets you outside. Choose from: Post Waffle Crisp, Grape-Nuts Flakes, Bran Flakes; Kellogg's Complete Bran Flakes, Common Sense Oat Bran; General Mills Wheaties, Whole Grain Total.

1 (8-ounce) can crushed pineapple, undrained

1 cup milk (approximately)

½ cup applesauce

¼ cup vegetable oil

1 cup all-purpose flour

½ cup finely crushed cereal

2 tablespoons toasted wheat germ

¼ cup finely chopped walnuts or pecans

1 tablespoon baking powder

¼ teaspoon salt

2 egg whites, stiffly beaten

HONEY BUTTER SAUCE

1 cup honey

¼ cup butter or margarine

1 (3-inch) cinnamon stick

Reserved pineapple

1. Drain the pineapple, reserving the juice and pineapple separately. Add enough milk to the pineapple juice to measure 1½ cups. Add the applesauce and oil to the milk mixture. Blend well.

2. Combine the flour, cereal, wheat germ, nuts, baking powder, and salt. Add the milk mixture and stir until the dry ingredients are just moistened. Fold in the egg whites.

3. To make the Honey Butter Sauce, bring the honey, butter, cinnamon stick, and reserved pineapple to a boil in a small saucepan over medium-low heat, stirring constantly. Keep warm until serving.

4. Bake the waffles in a preheated, oiled waffle iron until golden (about 2 minutes). Serve with the Honey Butter Sauce.

Yield: 5 (5½ x 4½-inch) waffles

Raisin Bran Brunch Muffins

This batter will keep in the refrigerator for a week, and with all of its variations, you can be a muffin-of-the-day pro. Use Kellogg's Raisin Bran or 15 ounces of any other bran-flake cereal.

3 cups sugar

1 cup vegetable oil

4 large eggs

1 tablespoon plus 2 teaspoons baking soda

1½ teaspoons salt

1 quart buttermilk

5 cups all-purpose flour

1 (15-ounce) package cereal

1. Preheat the oven to 400°F.
2. Combine the sugar, oil, eggs, baking soda, and salt in a large mixing bowl. Beat with an electric mixer on medium speed until blended. Stir in the buttermilk.
3. Add the flour and cereal, stirring until the dry ingredients are moistened. Cover the batter tightly and store in the refrigerator up to 1 week. Do not stir before using.
4. When ready to bake, spoon the batter into muffin pans greased or lined with paper baking cups; fill three-fourths full. Bake for 16 to 18 minutes, or until a wooden toothpick inserted in the center comes out clean. Remove from the pans immediately.

Yield: about 4½ dozen

Spice Muffins: Add 1 tablespoon plus 1 teaspoon ground cinnamon to the batter.

Pineapple Muffins: Add 1 (20-ounce) can drained crushed pineapple to the batter when you stir in the cereal.

Fruit Cocktail Muffins: Add 1 (17-ounce) can drained fruit cocktail to the batter when you stir in the cereal.

Chocolate Chip Muffins: Add 1½ cups chocolate morsels to the batter when you stir in the cereal. Stir in 1 cup chopped pecans, if you like.

Apple Muffins: Substitute 2 cups applesauce for 2 cups buttermilk. Add 2 cups chopped, peeled apple and 1 tablespoon apple pie spice to the batter when you stir in the cereal.

House Blend

Have you ever squinted at the shelf in Jerry Seinfeld's TV set kitchen trying to figure out his favorites? Well, I've kept a running list. Sometimes it changes, but here's what appears most often: Post Honeycomb, Blueberry Morning, Alpha Bits; General Mills Raisin Nut Bran; Kellogg's Frosted Flakes.

Using a little deductive reasoning, here's how I imagine all that cereal gets consumed. Since Jerry obviously likes his health food with a little sugar he probably eats Honeycomb and Alpha Bits straight from the box. Frosted Flakes and Raisin Nut Bran get the milk treatment. Blueberry Morning tops frozen yogurt. And he dumps the ends of all the boxes together into his House Blend to save for:

A Snack for Sleepwalkers

1 pita bread round
Butter or margarine
Cinnamon sugar
2 tablespoons light cream cheese
House Blend (or your favorites, combined)

1. Preheat the oven to 350°F.

2. Separate the pita bread into 2 rounds. Butter one side of each round, place on a baking sheet, and sprinkle liberally with the cinnamon sugar. Bake for 5 to 10 minutes, or until lightly toasted. Dot with the cream cheese; place in the oven briefly to soften the cheese, then spread. Sprinkle House Blend over the cheese.

Yield: 2 servings

Overnight Refrigerator Grain Pancakes

Yeast adds a light texture to these pancakes. You can mix them up the night before, and since the batter will keep in the refrigerator for up to a week, you can have pancakes whenever you like without much trouble. If you have time to cook them all and you want to freeze some for future breakfasts, wrap them in plastic wrap in stacks of 3 to 5 and then place in a freezer bag. Use a whole box of Kellogg's Raisin Bran or Fruitful Bran.

1 package active dry yeast

¼ cup warm water (105° to 115°F)

2 cups whole wheat flour

3 tablespoons sugar

2 tablespoons baking powder

2 teaspoons baking soda

½ teaspoon salt

1 (15-ounce) box cereal

6 large eggs, or 1½ cups egg substitute

1 quart buttermilk, or 4 cups plain low-fat yogurt

¼ cup vegetable oil

1. Combine the yeast and warm water in a liquid measuring cup; let stand for 5 minutes.

2. Combine the flour, sugar, baking powder, baking soda, and salt in a large bowl; mix well. Stir in the cereal.

3. Beat the eggs, buttermilk, oil, and yeast mixture until blended; add to the flour mixture and stir until the dry ingredients are moistened. Cover and refrigerate for 8 hours or overnight. (The mixture can be stored in an airtight container in the refrigerator for up to 1 week.)

4. Remove the batter from the refrigerator and stir it. For each pancake, pour about ¼ cup batter into a heavy skillet over medium heat. Cook until the top is covered with bubbles and the edges look dry; turn and brown the other side.

Yield: about 20 pancakes

100% Brunch in a Casserole

This has got everything you want to eat for breakfast in it. For the topping, use: Post Bran Flakes, Grape-Nuts Flakes; Kellogg's Complete Bran Flakes; General Mills Whole Grain Total, Wheaties.

    1 cup finely diced ham or Canadian bacon

    ½ cup chopped green onion

    ⅓ cup butter or margarine, melted

    12 large eggs, beaten, or 3 (8-ounce) cartons egg substitute

    1 (10¾-ounce) can condensed nacho cheese or
        cheddar cheese soup, undiluted

    1 (4-ounce) can sliced mushrooms, drained

    1 (2-ounce) jar diced pimientos

    ¾ cup regular or light sour cream

    1½ cups crushed cereal

1. Sauté the ham and onion in 2 tablespoons of the butter in a large heavy skillet over medium-high heat for 4 minutes. Add the eggs; cook, without stirring, until the mixture begins to set on the bottom. Reduce the heat to medium; draw a spatula across the bottom of the skillet to form large curds. Continue until the eggs are thickened but still moist; do not stir constantly. Remove from the heat.

2. Combine the soup, mushrooms, pimientos, and sour cream; stir well. Stir gently into the egg mixture; spoon into a greased 12 x 8 x 2-inch baking dish.

3. Combine the cereal and the remaining melted butter; sprinkle evenly over the egg mixture. Cover and refrigerate for 8 hours or overnight.

4. Remove the mixture from the refrigerator; let stand for 30 minutes. Preheat oven to 350°F. Bake, uncovered, at 350°F for 30 minutes, or until hot.

Yield: 8 servings

Ham and Cheese Wheat Brunchwich

Tip: To reduce the calories and fat in this sandwich, use light mayonnaise, reduced-fat cheese, 1/2 cup egg substitute instead of eggs, skim or low-fat milk, and no-sugar-added strawberry fruit spread. For the best sandwich coating, use General Mills Whole Grain Total, Wheaties, or Wheaties Honey Gold.

¼ cup plus 1 tablespoon mayonnaise

3 tablespoons strawberry jam

1 tablespoon Dijon mustard

4 (¾-inch-thick) slices Italian bread

2 slices cooked ham or smoked turkey, cut to fit bread

2 slices Swiss or cheddar cheese, cut to fit bread

2 large eggs

¼ cup milk

¼ teaspoon salt

1 cup finely crushed cereal

2 tablespoons butter or margarine, melted

1. Mix together 1 tablespoon of the mayonnaise and the jam; set aside.

2. Combine 2 tablespoons of the mayonnaise and the mustard; spread the mixture evenly on both sides of each bread slice. For each sandwich, layer the ham and cheese on a slice of bread; top with another bread slice.

3. Beat the eggs, milk, the remaining 2 tablespoons mayonnaise, and the salt in a shallow dish; dredge the sandwiches in the mixture. Coat with the cereal, pressing it into the bread to adhere.

4. Melt the butter in a heavy medium skillet over medium heat. Add the sandwiches. Cook on both sides until browned and the cheese is melted. Serve with the jam mixture for dipping.

Yield: 2 servings

SQUARES

Buttermilk Wheat Biscuits or Crackers

There's only one cereal to use because it packs wheat flavor and absorbs liquid like whole wheat flour: Ralston Foods 100% Whole Grain Wheat Chex.

2½ cups cereal
2 cups all-purpose flour
1 tablespoon baking powder
1 tablespoon sugar
1 teaspoon baking soda
½ teaspoon salt
⅔ cup shortening or butter-flavored shortening,
    cut into small pieces
1 cup buttermilk

1. Preheat the oven to 400°F.
2. Place the cereal in a food processor and process until finely crushed. Add the flour, baking powder, sugar, baking soda, and salt; pulse until blended. Sprinkle the shortening over the flour mixture; pulse just until the mixture resembles fine crumbs.
3. Transfer to a large bowl. Stir the buttermilk into the flour mixture until a soft dough forms. Turn the dough out onto a floured surface; knead 10 times. Roll the dough out into an 8-inch square; cut into 16 (2-inch) squares. (Do not use a sawing motion; cut straight down into the dough.)
4. Place the biscuits on a baking sheet; bake for 25 to 28 minutes, or until browned and cooked. Serve warm.

Yield: 16 biscuits

Buttermilk Crackers: Divide the dough into 4 equal parts. Roll each into a 12 x 6-inch rectangle. Cut into 2-inch squares and place on a baking sheet. Bake at 400°F for 15 minutes, or until browned. Let cool before serving. Makes about 5 dozen crackers.

Rollin' in Dough

From the same dough you can make either biscuits or crackers. The biscuits have almost a melt-in-your-mouth texture, such as the ones that your grandmother used to make, but the whole wheat texture and flavor give them a '90s attitude. The crackers are so tasty that you won't need a topping. Serve them plain as a snack or enjoy them with a salad.

Pumpkin Wheat Muffins

If you need to grab a meal in a muffin, make sure it's a nutrition-packed one like this recipe. To get the wheat flavor, use Ralston Foods 100% Whole Grain Wheat Chex or Multi Bran Chex.

1¼ cups unbleached or regular all-purpose flour

1½ cups crushed cereal

¼ cup sugar

2 teaspoons baking powder

½ teaspoon baking soda

1 teaspoon ground cinnamon

½ teaspoon salt

½ teaspoon pumpkin or apple pie spice

2 large eggs, lightly beaten

⅔ cup canned pumpkin or unsweetened applesauce

½ cup buttermilk

¼ cup light molasses

¼ cup canola oil

½ cup raisins (optional)

1. Preheat the oven to 375°F.

2. Combine the flour, cereal, sugar, baking powder, baking soda, cinnamon, salt, and pumpkin pie spice in a large bowl. Set aside.

3. Stir together the eggs, pumpkin, buttermilk, molasses, and oil in a medium-size bowl. Add the pumpkin mixture and raisins, if desired, to the flour mixture, and stir until the dry ingredients are just blended.

4. Spoon the batter evenly into muffin cups coated with cooking spray. Bake for 20 to 25 minutes, or until a wooden toothpick inserted in the center comes out clean.

Yield: 1 dozen

The History of Cereal in a Nutshell

Breakfast cereal as we know it was born in Battle Creek, Michigan, at the turn of the century. Dr. John Kellogg ran the Battle Creek Medical and Surgical Sanitarium, a "spa" where the rich and famous, sick and hypochondriac, fat and thin could spend their money on a spartan, fad-at-the-time diet of bran, grapes, and zwieback. (His theory was that people needed to chew dry brittle food to keep their teeth in shape.) Flake cereal was an accident—a product of zwieback bread dough gone awry. One day the dough got stale before it was processed, which resulted in flaking. When baked, the flakes were light and crisp. They were an instant hit at the sanitarium, and in that first year the hospital sold 100,000 pounds of cereal.

Two other names of note were developing cereals at the same time: Charles W. Post who gave us Post Toasties, and Henry Perky who invented shredded wheat. Actually they all knew each other. Dr. Post was a patient of Dr. John Kellogg's, who was in competition to develop a flaking process with Henry Perky, a Denver lawyer.

Frosted Streusel French Toast

This one will wake you up. The streusel top comes from buttery shreds using: Nabisco Frosted Wheat Bites; Kellogg's Frosted Mini-Wheats, Frosted Mini-Wheats Bite Size, Healthy Choice from Kellogg's Multi-Grain Squares.

3 large eggs, lightly beaten

¾ cup milk, half-and-half, or evaporated skim milk

¼ cup sugar

½ teaspoon ground cinnamon

¼ teaspoon ground nutmeg

2 teaspoons vanilla extract

6 to 8 (1-inch-thick) slices Italian bread

1 cup crushed cereal

¼ cup butter or margarine, melted

1. Combine the eggs, milk, sugar, cinnamon, nutmeg, and vanilla in a medium-size bowl; mix well using a wire whisk. Fit the bread slices, sides touching, in an even layer in a well-buttered, 9-inch square baking dish; pour the egg mixture over the bread slices. Cover and refrigerate for 2 hours or overnight, turning the bread slices once.

2. Preheat the oven to 375°F.

3. Combine the cereal and butter; sprinkle over the bread slices. Bake for 30 minutes.

Yield: 4 to 6 servings

Quick Whole Wheat Bread

This is especially great for breakfast topped with butter or cream cheese and jam. For the best flavor, use hearty Ralston Foods 100% Whole Grain Wheat Chex or Multi Bran Chex.

2 cups crushed cereal
½ cup all-purpose flour
1¼ teaspoons baking powder
¾ teaspoon baking soda
¼ teaspoon salt
1 teaspoon ground cinnamon
¼ cup raisins (optional)
¾ cup buttermilk
⅓ cup honey
¼ cup vegetable oil
1 large egg, lightly beaten

1. Preheat the oven to 350°F.

2. Combine the cereal, flour, baking powder, baking soda, salt, and cinnamon in a large bowl; stir well. Add raisins, if desired, and toss.

3. In a separate bowl, stir together the buttermilk, honey, oil, and egg. Pour the milk mixture into the cereal mixture and stir until the dry ingredients are just moistened.

4. Spoon into an 8-inch round cake pan coated with cooking spray and dusted with flour. Bake for 35 minutes, or until a wooden toothpick inserted in the center comes out clean. Serve warm, cut into wedges.

Yield: 6 to 8 servings

Country Apple Pudding

For a moist, cakelike pudding, use Quaker Cinnamon Life, Life, or Oat Bran.

4 large eggs, beaten

1¾ cups firmly packed light brown sugar

¼ cup butter or margarine, melted

2 teaspoons vanilla extract

1¾ teaspoons baking powder

½ teaspoon salt

3 cups coarsely crushed cereal

3 cups finely chopped Granny Smith apples

1 cup chopped walnuts or pecans

2 tablespoons bourbon or brandy (optional)

½ teaspoon apple pie spice

1. Preheat the oven to 325°F.

2. Combine the eggs, brown sugar, butter, vanilla, baking powder, and salt in a large mixing bowl; stir well. Stir in the cereal, apples, nuts, bourbon, if desired, and apple pie spice. Let stand for 15 minutes; stir well.

3. Pour the batter into a greased shallow 2-quart baking dish. Bake for 45 minutes. Serve warm with whipped cream or ice cream.

Yield: 6 to 8 servings

I f you lived in colonial times, you might have dumped that popcorn into a bowl and garnished it with cream, sugar, and fruit. As early America's first breakfast cereal, it was a little more difficult to prepare in those days: popcorn was cooked in the family fireplace in what resembles a fish grill-basket with a smaller grate.

SHREDS

Lemon Shredded Coffee Cake

Serve this moist cake freshly baked and warm for breakfast or brunch, drizzled with sweet yogurt icing. Any of the following cereals adds a slight wheat flavor and a dense, coffee-cake texture: Nabisco Shredded Wheat, Shredded Wheat Spoon Size, Shredded Wheat 'N Bran; Healthy Choice from Kellogg's Multi Grain Squares.

1½ cups all-purpose flour
1 cup finely crushed cereal
1 cup sugar
1 teaspoon baking soda
¼ teaspoon salt
⅔ cup plus 2 tablespoons lemon yogurt
¼ cup plus 2 tablespoons butter or margarine, melted
1 tablespoon grated lemon rind
1 tablespoon fresh lemon juice
1½ cups powdered sugar

1. Preheat the oven to 350°F.
2. Combine the flour, cereal, sugar, baking soda, and salt in a large bowl; mix well.
3. In a separate bowl, combine ⅔ cup of the yogurt, ¼ cup of the butter, the lemon rind, and lemon juice. Add to the dry ingredients and stir until moistened. Spread in a greased 9-inch square baking pan.
4. Bake for 28 to 30 minutes, or until a wooden toothpick inserted in the center comes out clean. Let cool in the pan on a wire rack.
5. Beat the powdered sugar, the remaining 2 tablespoons butter, and the remaining 2 tablespoons yogurt in a small bowl until smooth. Spread the icing over the cake and refrigerate to set.

Yield: 12 to 15 servings

Tuscan Shredded Wheat Bread

This chewy, dense loaf gets its crisp crust by cooking in a hot oven in a bath of steam. Use a food processor to finely crush the cereal. Choose from Nabisco Shredded Wheat Spoon Size, Shredded Wheat, or Shredded Wheat 'N Bran.

> 2 packages active dry yeast
> ¾ cup plus 2 tablespoons warm water (105° to 115°F)
> ½ cup milk, at room temperature
> ¼ cup honey
> 3 tablespoons olive oil
> 2 to 3 cups bread flour
> ½ cup whole wheat flour
> 1¼ cups finely shredded cereal
> ¾ cup chopped walnuts, lightly toasted
> 1 teaspoon salt

1. Combine the yeast and warm water in a 2-cup liquid measuring cup; let stand for 5 minutes. Stir in the milk, honey, and oil. Set aside.

2. Combine 2 cups of the bread flour, the whole wheat flour, ¾ cup of the cereal, the nuts, and salt in a large bowl; gradually add the yeast mixture, stirring until blended.

3. Turn the dough out onto a well-floured surface and knead until smooth and elastic (approximately 10 minutes), adding as much of the remaining 1 cup flour as needed to prevent sticking. Place the dough in a well-greased bowl and turn to grease the top. Cover and let rise in a warm (85°F), draft-free place for 1 hour, or until doubled in bulk.

4. Punch down the dough; shape it into a round. Roll the dough in the remaining ½ cup cereal, coating evenly. If desired, use a sharp knife to cut two ½-inch-deep crosswise slashes in the top of the loaf. Place on a greased baking sheet; cover lightly and let rise about 1 hour or until doubled in bulk.

5. Preheat the oven to 450°F.

6. Place a shallow pan of boiling water on the bottom rack of the oven. Spritz a light coating of water on the bread, and place the baking sheet in the lower third of the oven. Bake for 10 minutes; reduce the oven temperature to 350°F and bake for 35 to 40 additional minutes, or until the bread is well browned.

Yield: 1 loaf

A Box a Day

Because there are so many varieties of cereal to choose from, you could easily eat a different cereal each morning for a year. As a matter of fact, an average of two new ready-to-eat cereals are introduced each week. (The only reason there are no more than that introduced is the lack of available shelving at grocery stores. Ever notice there is one entire aisle devoted to cereal? And it's completely jammed with boxes.)

Frosted Wheat Pastry Twists

Frozen puff pastry thaws quickly if you leave it at room temperature. Nabisco Frosted Wheat Bites, Kellogg's Frosted Mini-Wheats Bite Size, or Healthy Choice from Kellogg's Multi-Grain Squares adds a crispy texture and will hold up beautifully during baking.

1 sheet frozen puff pastry, thawed
1 egg white, beaten
1 tablespoon water
½ cup finely crushed cereal
¼ cup firmly packed brown sugar
½ teaspoon ground cinnamon

1. Preheat the oven to 375°F.

2. Roll the pastry sheet on a lightly floured surface into a 14 x 11-inch rectangle. Beat together the egg white and water; brush on the pastry. Combine the cereal, brown sugar, and cinnamon; sprinkle evenly over the pastry. Gently press the cereal mixture into the pastry or roll with a rolling pin to adhere.

3. Cut the pastry sheet crosswise into ¾-inch-wide strips. Shape into twists and place on a greased baking sheet, pressing down the ends. Bake for 15 minutes, or until crisp and browned.

Yield: 18 twists

Crispy Cheese Puffs: Roll out the pastry sheet and brush with the egg white mixture as directed above. Mix ½ cup crushed Nabisco Shredded Wheat or Shredded Wheat Spoon Size with ¼ cup grated Parmesan cheese, 1 teaspoon freshly ground pepper, and 1 teaspoon Italian seasoning, if desired. Sprinkle over the pastry sheet and proceed as above.

THE GOOD STUFF

Hawaiian Banana Banana Bread

Post Banana Nut Crunch makes this rich, moist banana bread a doubleheader.

2½ cups all-purpose flour

2 cups cereal

2 cups sugar

1 teaspoon baking soda

½ teaspoon salt

1 teaspoon ground cinnamon

3 large eggs, beaten

¾ cup vegetable oil

2 cups mashed ripe bananas

1 (8-ounce) can crushed pineapple, undrained

2 teaspoons vanilla extract

1. Preheat the oven to 350°F.

2. Combine the flour, cereal, sugar, baking soda, salt, and cinnamon in a large bowl; mix well. Stir together the eggs, oil, banana, pineapple, and vanilla in a separate bowl; add to the flour mixture and stir until the dry ingredients are moistened.

3. Pour the batter into 2 greased and floured 8½ x 4½ x 3-inch loaf pans. Bake for 65 to 70 minutes, or until a wooden toothpick inserted in the center comes out clean. Cover loosely with foil after 30 minutes of baking to prevent overbrowning. Let cool for 10 minutes. Remove from the pans and let cool on wire racks. The loaves may be stored in the freezer for up to 1 month.

Yield: 2 loaves

Carrot Cake
Temptation Muffins
and Cupcakes

When you add one of the following cereals to these muffins, you get more flavor than you've ever had in a carrot muffin: Kellogg's Temptations French Vanilla Almond, Temptations Honey Roasted Pecan, Nut & Honey Crunch; Quaker Toasted Oatmeal Honey Nut; Post Honey Bunches of Oats with Almonds; General Mills Oatmeal Crisp Almond.

1½ cups all-purpose flour

½ cup sugar

1 tablespoon baking powder

½ teaspoon salt

½ teaspoon ground cinnamon

1½ cups cereal

1½ cups finely shredded carrot

⅔ cup milk

¼ cup vegetable oil

2 large eggs, beaten

1. Preheat the oven to 400°F.

2. Combine the flour, sugar, baking powder, salt, cinnamon, and cereal in a large bowl; mix well. Combine the carrot, milk, oil, and eggs in a separate bowl, then stir this mixture into the bowl of dry ingredients until just moistened.

3. Spoon the batter evenly into 10 greased (2½-inch) muffin cups (fill the empty muffin cups with a little water to prevent scorching). Bake for 15 to 20 minutes, or until a wooden toothpick inserted in the center comes out clean.

Yield: 10 muffins

To make these muffins into cupcakes, spread the cooled surface with this frosting.

PINEAPPLE FROSTING

2¾ to 3 cups sifted powdered sugar

3 tablespoons softened butter or margarine

¼ cup drained crushed pineapple

Beat 2 cups of the powdered sugar and the butter until blended; beat in pineapple until fluffy. Add remaining powdered sugar to make frosting spreadable.

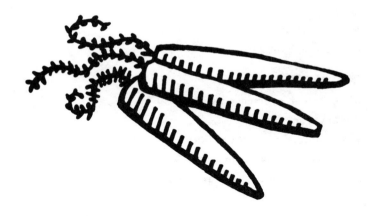

Chocolate Chip
Banana Crunch Muffins

Decorate with chocolate morsels or sprinkle with additional cereal, if desired. Post Banana Nut Crunch will double your banana pleasure in these muffins, and Honey Bunches of Oats or General Mills Clusters will add a delicious honey crunch. Add any one of these cereals to the cakelike batter along with chocolate morsels, and you'll end up with a wonderful, moist muffin.

1½ cups all-purpose flour

1 tablespoon baking powder

¼ teaspoon baking soda

½ teaspoon salt

1½ cups cereal

½ cup semisweet chocolate mini morsels

1 medium very ripe banana (about ½ cup)

⅓ cup sugar

⅔ cup milk

¼ cup vegetable oil

1 large egg, lightly beaten

CRUMBLE TOPPING

¾ cup cereal, coarsely crushed

¼ cup sugar

3 tablespoons all-purpose flour

½ teaspoon ground cinnamon

2 tablespoons butter or margarine, melted

1. Preheat the oven to 400°F.

2. Combine the flour, baking powder, baking soda, salt, cereal, and chocolate in a large bowl; stir well. Combine the banana, sugar, milk, oil, and egg in a separate bowl; mix well, using a wire whisk. Add to the cereal mixture and stir until the dry ingredients are just moistened. Spoon into 12 greased 2½-inch muffin cups.

3. To make the Crumble Topping, combine all of the ingredients in a medium-size bowl; mix well. Sprinkle over the muffin.

4. Bake for 18 to 20 minutes, or until a wooden toothpick inserted in the center comes out clean.

Yield: 1 dozen

A Truly Amazing Muffin

I make these with the crunch topping, or I'll sometimes frost the muffins with peanut butter mixed with a little powdered sugar until smooth. If I'm feeling indecisive, I'll make crunch-topped muffins and mix up the peanut butter stuff, which I'll eat with every bite.

Double Blueberry Morning Muffins

These moist muffins get a double dose of blueberries from the muffin mix and the 1½ cups Post Blueberry Morning mixed in. Add ½ cup Kellogg's Cracklin' Oat Bran to the packet of topping to make a tasty, crunchy crumble that is sprinkled on the muffins before baking.

> ¾ cup milk
> 3 tablespoons lemon juice
> 3 egg whites
> 1½ cups cereal
> 1 (23.5-ounce) package Duncan Hines Bakery Style
>   Blueberry Muffin Mix with Crumb Topping
> ½ cup crushed cereal
> ½ cup sifted powdered sugar

1. Combine the milk, 2 tablespoons of the lemon juice, the egg whites, and 1½ cups cereal in a large bowl; mix well. Let stand for 5 minutes at room temperature and then stir.

2. Pour the muffin mix into a large fine wire-mesh sieve or sifter; sift into the bowl of cereal mixture. Stir until the dry ingredients are just moistened. Fold in the rinsed and well-drained blueberries. Pour into greased and floured or paper-lined muffin pans.

3. Combine the contents of the topping packet with the crushed cereal; sprinkle over the batter. Bake as directed on the package. Let cool in the pans for 10 minutes.

4. Stir together the powdered sugar and the remaining 1 tablespoon lemon juice; drizzle over the muffins.

Yield: 1 dozen

Bran Gingerbread

A low-fat, yet tender version; bran cereal gives it rich flavor. Try Kellogg's All-Bran, General Mills Fiber One, or Nabisco 100% Bran.

1 cup cereal
½ cup sugar
¾ cup buttermilk
½ cup canned pumpkin or applesauce
½ cup molasses
½ cup egg substitute, or 2 large eggs, lightly beaten
2 tablespoons vegetable oil
1½ cups all-purpose flour
1½ teaspoons ground ginger
1 teaspoon baking soda
½ teaspoon ground cinnamon
¼ teaspoon salt
¼ teaspoon ground cloves

1. Preheat the oven to 350°F.

2. Combine the cereal, sugar, buttermilk, pumpkin, molasses, egg substitute, and oil in a large bowl; stir well. Let stand for 10 minutes.

3. Combine the flour, ginger, baking soda, cinnamon, salt, and cloves; mix well. Add to the cereal mixture and stir until the dry ingredients are just moistened. Pour into a greased and floured 9-inch square baking pan; bake for 35 minutes, or until a wooden toothpick inserted in the center comes out clean.

4. Cut into squares; serve warm or at room temperature with frozen vanilla yogurt or light whipped topping, if desired.

Yield: 9 to 12 servings

Lemon Blueberry Bran Bread

Kellogg's Cracklin' Oat Bran turns the crumb topping in this mix into a crunchy streusel.

> ¾ cup skim milk
> 3 tablespoons lemon juice
> 1 tablespoon grated lemon rind
> 3 egg whites
> 2 cups crushed cereal
> 1 (23.5-ounce) package Duncan Hines Bakery Style
>   Blueberry Muffin Mix with Crumb Topping
> ½ cup sifted powdered sugar

1. Preheat the oven to 350°F.

2. Combine the milk, 2 tablespoons of the lemon juice, the lemon rind, egg whites, and 1½ cups of the cereal in a large bowl; mix well. Let stand for 15 minutes at room temperature; stir.

3. Pour the muffin mix into a large fine wire-mesh sieve or sifter; sift into the bowl of cereal mixture. Stir until the dry ingredients are just moistened. Fold in the rinsed and well-drained blueberries. Pour into a greased and floured 9 x 5 x 3-inch loaf pan.

4. Combine the contents of the topping packet with the remaining ½ cup cereal; sprinkle over the batter. Bake for 55 to 60 minutes, or until a wooden toothpick inserted in the center comes out clean. Cool in the pan for 10 minutes. Remove from the pan and let cool completely on a wire rack.

5. Stir together the powdered sugar and the remaining 1 tablespoon lemon juice; drizzle over the loaf.

Yield: 1 loaf

The Complete Breakfast Pizza

You get the breakfast basics in this: ham, cheese, eggs, and cereal. I love the way little cereal flakes get crunchy when you mix them with butter and sprinkle them on top of this tasty brunch pie; use Post Great Grains Crunchy Pecan or General Mills Basic 4.

> 3 cups cereal
>
> 2 cups reduced-fat or regular baking mix like Bisquick
>
> 1 teaspoon sugar
>
> ½ cup milk
>
> 1 cup finely chopped ham
>
> ½ cup sliced green onion (optional)
>
> 4 hard-boiled eggs, sliced
>
> 1 cup (4 ounces) shredded cheddar or Swiss cheese
>
> 2 tablespoons butter or margarine, melted

1. Preheat the oven to 375°F.

2. Combine 2 cups of the cereal, the baking mix, sugar, and milk, stirring until a soft dough forms. Turn the dough out onto a surface lightly dusted with baking mix; knead gently 10 times. Press the dough (with moistened or greased hands) into the bottom of an 11 x 7 x 1-inch baking pan or 12-inch pizza pan. Bake for 10 minutes on the lowest rack of the oven. Let cool.

3. Sprinkle the ham, onion, if desired, egg slices, and cheese over the dough. Combine the remaining 1 cup cereal and the butter; sprinkle over the layered ingredients. Bake for 5 to 10 minutes, or until the cheese melts.

Yield: 6 to 8 servings

Hearty Bran Nut Bread

This hearty loaf is delicious sliced, heated, and served with cream cheese for breakfast. These cereals will give it hearty flavor: Kellogg's All-Bran, All-Bran Extra Fiber; General Mills Fiber One; Nabisco 100% Bran.

1 cup cereal

1 cup firmly packed light brown sugar

1 cup buttermilk

1 large egg, lightly beaten

1 cup all-purpose flour

1 teaspoon baking powder

½ teaspoon baking soda

¼ teaspoon salt

1½ cups chopped walnuts

1. Preheat the oven to 350°F.

2. Combine the cereal, brown sugar, buttermilk, and egg in a large bowl; mix well. Let stand for 15 minutes; stir well.

3. Combine the flour, baking powder, baking soda, and salt in a separate bowl. Add the nuts and stir into the cereal mixture until the dry ingredients are moistened. Spread in a greased and floured 9 x 5 x 3-inch loaf pan.

4. Bake for 55 minutes, or until a wooden toothpick inserted in the center comes out clean. Let cool in the pan for 10 minutes; remove from the pan and cool completely on a wire rack.

Yield: 1 loaf

Red, White, and Blue Granola Parfait

Yogurt is quickly thickened to give the creamy layers of this healthy "sundae" more body. These cereals will hold up under the fruit and yogurt: Kellogg's Low Fat Granola without Raisins; Quaker Sun Country Granola with Almonds, 100% Natural Granola Oats & Honey. I love the flavor with Post Blueberry Morning, but you'll need to eat the parfait immediately if you make it with this cereal.

1 (8-ounce) container vanilla-flavored yogurt
½ cup powdered sugar
1 (10-ounce) package frozen raspberries *or* strawberries in light syrup,
    thawed
4 cups frozen whipped topping, thawed, or sweetened whipped cream
1⅓ cups fresh blueberries
1⅓ cups cereal

1. Spread the yogurt ½-inch thick on several layers of paper towels; place 2 layers of paper towels on top of the yogurt. Let stand for 15 minutes; using a rubber spatula, scrape the yogurt from the paper towels into a large bowl. Stir in the powdered sugar.

2. Puree the raspberries in an electric blender; strain through a wire sieve into a bowl, pressing down hard on the solids. Stir the raspberry puree into the yogurt mixture; fold in the whipped topping.

3. Spoon half of the mixture into 4 (8- to 12-ounce) stemmed glasses; sprinkle with half of the blueberries and cereal. Repeat the layers. Serve immediately, or cover and refrigerate for 2 hours.

Yield: 4 servings

Don't Think, Just Cook

Flakes

Commonsense Country Oat Squash Casserole
Mexican Turkey Burgers
Unfried Green Tomatoes, Etc.
Toasty Fried Cheese Marinara
Flaky 4-Ingredient Honey Mustard Chicken
Totally Spicy Hot Wings
King of Crunch Tenders

Squares

Wheat Grain Black Bean Burgers
Crispy Crust Tuna Family Supper
Chicken Nacho Supper in a Bowl
Creamy Double Corn Casserole
Italian Seasoned Roasted Vegetables
Crispy Cheese Wafers

Shreds

Oven-Crusted Potatoes

The Good Stuff

Pear Streusel Acorn Squash
Blender Lunch Box Bran Muffins

FLAKES

Commonsense Country Oat Squash Casserole

This is great as a quick dinner by itself, or serve with baked or grilled chicken during the summer and roast turkey or pork tenderloin during the winter. The cereal replaces crackers, so your casserole won't be thick and gummy. Try Kellogg's Common Sense Oat Bran, Corn Flakes, Toasted Corn Flakes; General Mills Wheaties, Whole Grain Total, Country Corn Flakes, Total Corn Flakes; Post Toasties.

¼ cup margarine or butter, melted

1½ cups crushed cereal

2 pounds yellow squash, cut into ½-inch-thick slices

1 (8-ounce) can sliced water chestnuts, drained

½ cup mayonnaise or light sour cream

½ teaspoon dried basil

¼ teaspoon salt

½ teaspoon freshly ground pepper

1½ cups (6 ounces) shredded cheddar cheese

1. Preheat the oven to 400°F.

2. Combine 2 tablespoons of the butter and the cereal, mixing thoroughly. Set aside.

3. Sauté the squash in the remaining 2 tablespoons butter in a large heavy skillet for 20 minutes, or until tender. Stir in the water chestnuts, mayonnaise, basil, salt, and pepper. Set aside.

4. Spoon the squash evenly into a greased, 1½-quart shallow baking dish; sprinkle with ¾ cup of the cheese and then half of the cereal mixture. Repeat the layers. Bake, uncovered, for 15 to 20 minutes, or until hot.

Yield: 6 servings

Mexican Turkey Burgers

Flakes made from corn give these easy, hearty burgers a more authentic flavor: Post Toasties; Kellogg's Corn Flakes, Toasted Corn Flakes; General Mills Country Corn Flakes, Total Corn Flakes.

¾ pound ground turkey

¼ pound chorizo sausage, casings removed, or bulk pork sausage

1 cup finely crushed cereal

1 (10-ounce) can diced tomatoes and green chilies, drained

GUACAMOLE

1 medium, ripe avocado, seeded and peeled

1 tablespoon lemon or lime juice

¼ cup minced green onion

¼ teaspoon garlic salt

¼ teaspoon Tabasco or other hot sauce

6 lettuce leaves

6 hamburger buns, split and toasted

1. Combine the turkey, sausage, cereal, and tomatoes and green chilies in a bowl; mix well. Shape the mixture into 6 patties ¾-inch thick.

2. To prepare the guacamole, mash the avocado with lemon juice; stir in the onion, garlic salt, and hot sauce.

3. Cook the patties in a nonstick skillet over medium heat for 8 to 12 minutes, or until cooked, flipping once. Or place the patties on a large piece of heavy-duty aluminum foil and put on a grill. Cover with the grill lid and cook over medium-hot coals (350° to 400°F) for 7 to 8 minutes on each side. Serve in lettuce-lined buns with the guacamole.

Yield: 6 servings

Note: If you wish to substitute for the sausage, use a total of 1 pound ground turkey and add 2 tablespoons Mexican chili powder seasoning (not chili powder) to the mixture.

Unfried Green Tomatoes, Etc.

Here's a way to get the flavor without the fat. Try eating these with a slice of provolone cheese on top of a hamburger in a bun: yum. Kellogg's Toasted Corn Flakes, General Mills Total Corn Flakes, and General Mills Country Corn Flakes are sturdier than regular cornflakes and will make a crispier coating.

Note: *To keep cooked tomatoes, zucchini, and eggplant from getting soggy before you serve them, stand them up like wheels in the serving dish after all are cooked instead of stacking them.*

1 egg, beaten
½ cup milk or buttermilk
2½ cups cereal
½ cup self-rising flour
6 green tomatoes, or 3 large zucchini, or 2 small eggplants,
    cut into ½-inch-thick slices
Vegetable cooking spray

1. Preheat the oven to 400°F.

2. Mix the egg and milk in a shallow dish. Combine the cereal and the flour in a food processor and process until the cereal is finely crushed. Transfer to another shallow dish.

3. Working in batches, dip the vegetable slices into the egg mixture, allowing the excess to drip back into the dish. Coat both sides with the cornflake mixture, pressing to adhere. Place on a greased large wire cooling rack set in a jelly roll pan. Coat the tops of the slices with cooking spray.

4. Bake for 20 to 30 minutes, or until browned and tender, flipping once and coating the tops with cooking spray.

Yield: 4 to 6 servings

Toasty Fried Cheese Marinara

Serve as an appetizer or on top of mixed greens dressed with a vinaigrette. You can bake or fry these cubes; frying yields a crispier crust with a hint of olive oil. If you decide to bake them, a coating of olive oil–flavored cooking spray keeps the crust from appearing dry and flaky and gives more flavor. Adel DaVinci Italian Seasoning works well, but any Italian seasoning-salt mixture will work, and you can always mix 1 teaspoon dried Italian herbs with ½ teaspoon salt. These mild-tasting flake cereals hold their texture: Kellogg's Toasted Corn Flakes; General Mills Country Corn Flakes, Total Corn Flakes.

4 cups cereal

1 teaspoon Italian seasoning

½ teaspoon cayenne

8 ounces Gruyère or mozzarella cheese, cut into 1-inch cubes

½ cup all-purpose flour

3 large eggs

2 tablespoons water

Olive oil for deep frying

2 cups commercial refrigerated marinara sauce

1. Combine the cereal, Italian seasoning, and cayenne in a food processor and process until fine crumbs form. Transfer to a shallow dish.

2. Toss the cheese cubes with the flour in a large bowl; remove from the flour, shaking the excess back into the bowl. Beat the eggs and water in a shallow dish. Dip the cheese cubes into the egg mixture and then roll in the cereal mixture, pressing firmly to adhere. Carefully repeat the dipping process to coat well. Place on a baking sheet; refrigerate for at least 1 hour and up to 4 hours before frying or baking.

3. Fry the cheese cubes in 2 inches hot olive oil (375°F) in a deep skillet until golden brown. Drain on paper towels. Or bake in a preheated oven at 400°F for 8 to 10 minutes, or until golden brown and the cheese starts to melt. Serve immediately with the marinara sauce for dipping.

Yield: about 2 dozen

Note: Cheddar, provolone, or Monterey Jack cheese may be substituted.

Flaky 4-Ingredient Honey Mustard Chicken

Use these cereals for a crunchy crust: Post Toasties; Kellogg's Product 19, Toasted Corn Flakes, Corn Flakes; General Mills Country Corn Flakes, Total Corn Flakes.

½ cup dry-roasted or honey-roasted peanuts
¾ cup cereal
4 chicken breast halves, skinned and boned
½ cup commercial honey mustard plus additional for serving

1. Preheat oven to 400°F.

2. Place the peanuts in a food processor and pulse until finely chopped. Add the cereal; pulse until the mixture resembles crumbs. Transfer to a piece of waxed paper.

3. Coat each chicken breast with the honey mustard and then roll in the crumb mixture, coating well. Place in a greased shallow baking dish; bake for 20 to 25 minutes, or until cooked through, turning once. Serve with additional honey mustard.

Yield: 4 servings

Totally Spicy Hot Wings

Chicken wings may be America's favorite bar food, but you don't have to head to the nearest bar to get them. These are ultrasimple to prepare. Cornflakes make a crispy coating: Kellogg's Corn Flakes, Toasted Corn Flakes; General Mills Country Corn Flakes, Whole Grain Total, Total Corn Flakes. Serve them with taco or picante sauce or with salsa, guacamole, and sour cream for dipping.

2 pounds chicken drummettes
½ cup buttermilk
1 to 2 tablespoons Tabasco or other hot sauce
1½ cups finely crushed cereal
1 (1.25-ounce) package taco seasoning mix

1. Combine the chicken, buttermilk, and hot sauce in a plastic bag. Make sure the drummettes are coated with the liquid; then seal the bag and refrigerate for 1 hour.

2. Preheat the oven to 375°F.

3. Combine the cereal and taco seasoning mix in a shallow dish. Dredge the drummettes in the cereal mixture. Place in a lightly greased jelly roll pan.

4. Bake for 30 to 35 minutes, or until browned, turning once.

Yield: 8 to 10 appetizer servings

King of Crunch Tenders

If there's anything absolutely everyone will eat for dinner, it's chicken fingers. I've fed them to my daughter's Brownie troop and to the children my friends bring over while we eat "gourmet" food. (The adults always sneak a few.) People are always asking me for this recipe. Use 4 cups of Quaker Cap'n Crunch cereal and 3 cups of any of the following: Post Toasties; Kellogg's Corn Flakes; General Mills Country Corn Flakes, Total Corn Flakes.

    4 cups Cap'n Crunch

    3 cups cornflake cereal

    1½ cups all-purpose flour

    1 teaspoon onion powder

    ½ teaspoon seasoned salt

    ½ teaspoon pepper

    3 large eggs

    ¼ cup milk

    1½ pounds chilled chicken tenders or skinned and boned chicken
        breast halves, cut lengthwise into 2-inch-wide strips

    Vegetable oil for deep frying

1. Process the cereals in a food processor until crumbled but with some remaining ⅛-inch chunks. Spread in a shallow dish. Combine the flour, onion powder, seasoned salt, and pepper in a shallow dish. Combine the eggs and milk in a separate shallow dish, beating until blended.

2. Dredge the chicken tenders in the flour mixture; roll in the egg mixture, and then dredge in the cereal mixture, pressing to adhere and coat well. Arrange on a baking sheet lined with waxed paper. Refrigerate until ready to fry.

3. Heat the oil in a deep fryer to 325°F, or heat 3 inches of oil in a large heavy skillet to 325°F. Fry the chicken in batches for 3½ minutes, or until golden, turning once if using a skillet. Drain on paper towels.

Yield: 4 to 6 servings

SQUARES

Wheat Grain Black Bean Burgers

Fresh fruit salad will taste refreshing beside this Southwest-style meatless burger. Use a big-flavored cereal such as Ralston Foods 100% Whole Grain Wheat Chex or Multi Bran Chex.

> 1 (15- to 16-ounce) can black beans, rinsed and drained
> ½ cup finely crushed cereal
> ⅓ cup finely chopped red onion
> 3 tablespoons picante sauce
> 1 teaspoon ground cumin
> ½ teaspoon salt
> 4 hamburger buns
>
> TOPPINGS: salsa, guacamole, sliced avocado, sour cream,
>   sliced ripe olives, sprouts

1. Mash the beans with a potato masher in a medium bowl. Stir in the cereal, onion, picante sauce, cumin, and salt. Shape into 4 (¾-inch-thick) patties.

2. Place the patties on a greased baking sheet; broil 4 to 5 inches from the heat source for 3 to 4 minutes on each side, or until lightly browned. Serve in the warmed buns with the desired toppings.

Yield: 4 servings

Crispy Crust
Tuna Family Supper

Cereal takes the place of cracker crumbs to make this casserole thick and yummy and the topping crisp. Try: Kellogg's Crispix; Ralston Foods Corn Chex, Double Chex, Rice Chex, 100% Whole Grain Wheat Chex, Multi Bran Chex. For a lighter version, use reduced-fat, reduced-sodium cream of mushroom soup, reduced-fat sour cream, and reduced-fat mayonnaise.

2 (6⅛-ounce) cans solid white tuna packed in water, drained and flaked

1 (8-ounce) can sliced water chestnuts, drained

2½ cups coarsely crushed cereal

1 cup sliced celery

½ cup sliced green onion

½ cup chopped cashews or toasted slivered almonds

1 (10¾-ounce) can cream of mushroom soup, undiluted

1 cup sour cream

⅓ cup plus 2 tablespoons grated Parmesan cheese

½ cup mayonnaise

1 teaspoon Tabasco or other hot sauce (optional)

1 tablespoon butter or margarine, melted

1. Preheat the oven to 350°F.

2. Combine the tuna, water chestnuts, 1 cup of the cereal, the celery, onion, and nuts; mix well. In a separate bowl, stir together the soup, sour cream, ⅓ cup of the cheese, the mayonnaise, and hot sauce, if desired; mix well. Stir into the tuna mixture.

3. Spread in a shallow 2-quart baking dish coated with cooking spray. Cover with foil and bake for 30 minutes. Meanwhile, combine the remaining 1½ cups cereal, the remaining 2 tablespoons Parmesan cheese, and the butter. Remove the foil from the casserole and sprinkle with the cereal topping. Bake for 10 more minutes, or until crisp.

Yield: 4 to 6 servings

Chicken Nacho Supper
in a Bowl

Eat these individual bowls of nachos with a spoon. Use Quaker Crunchy Corn Bran;
Ralston Foods Corn Chex, Double Chex; or Kellogg's Crispix as the crunchy base.

8 ounces reduced-fat or regular American cheese spread, such as
   Healthy Choice or Velveeta, cubed

1 (10-ounce) can diced tomatoes and green chilies, drained

1½ cups shredded cooked chicken

3 cups cereal

1½ cups shredded lettuce

½ cup thinly sliced black olives

TOPPINGS: sour cream, guacamole, salsa

1. Combine the cheese, tomatoes and chilies, and chicken in a heavy saucepan.
   Cook over low heat, stirring constantly, until hot and the cheese is melted.
   Or combine the ingredients in a glass bowl; cover and microwave on HIGH
   for 3½ to 4 minutes, or until the cheese melts, stirring after 2 minutes.

2. Place ¾ cup of the cereal in each of 4 shallow soup bowls; spoon the cheese
   mixture evenly over the cereal. Sprinkle the lettuce and olives on top, and
   serve immediately with the desired toppings.

Yield: 4 servings

Creamy Double Corn Casserole

Using a food processor to puree the corn releases its natural starch and sugars, so this dish tastes almost like polenta. Use Ralston Foods Corn Chex for double the corn taste.

3 cups fresh or frozen thawed corn kernels

½ cup chopped onion

1 cup milk

3 cups cereal

2 large eggs

3 tablespoons butter or margarine, melted

1 tablespoon sugar

½ teaspoon salt

¼ teaspoon cayenne

1. Preheat the oven to 350°F.

2. Combine the corn, onion, and ½ cup of the milk in a food processor and process until the mixture is coarsely pureed. Pour into a large bowl. Add the cereal, eggs, butter, sugar, salt, cayenne, and the remaining ½ cup milk to the food processor; process until smooth. Add to the corn mixture and stir well.

3. Pour into a greased 9-inch square baking dish. Bake for 35 to 40 minutes, or until set.

Yield: 6 to 8 servings

Italian Seasoned Roasted Vegetables

Roasting vegetables in the oven seems so much easier to me than steaming, when you want them to turn out crisp, tender, and intensely flavored. This seasoned crispy coating makes them even tastier. They are wonderful to serve at cookouts with hamburgers or grilled chicken, or even as an appetizer for a party.

Roll the vegetables in one of these cereals: Kellogg's Crispix; Ralston Foods Double Chex, Corn Chex.

> 2 cups finely crushed cereal
> 1 (0.7-ounce) envelope Good Seasons Italian Salad Dressing Mix
> 6 cups assorted vegetables: broccoli florets, carrot slices, cauliflorets,
>   red bell pepper strips, yellow squash slices, zucchini slices
> ⅔ cup regular or reduced-calorie mayonnaise

1. Preheat the oven to 450°F.

2. Combine the cereal and salad dressing mix in a shallow bowl. Combine the vegetables and mayonnaise in a large bowl; toss gently until the vegetables are well coated with the mayonnaise.

3. Dredge the coated vegetables in the cereal mixture and arrange in a single layer on an ungreased baking sheet; make sure the pieces do not touch. Bake for 10 minutes, or until golden brown.

Yield: 6 to 8 servings

Crispy Cheese Wafers

These crispy little silver-dollar cheese wafers are even crispier when you use Chex cereals in the mix: Ralston Foods 100% Whole Grain Wheat Chex, Multi Bran Chex, or Corn Chex. You can freeze them after baking and reheat by placing the frozen wafers on a baking sheet and heating at 350°F for 10 to 15 minutes.

1 cup all-purpose flour
½ teaspoon garlic salt or Cajun seasoning
¼ to ½ teaspoon cayenne
½ cup margarine, softened and cut into pieces
1 cup (4 ounces) shredded sharp cheddar cheese
2 cups crushed cereal
1 egg white
1 tablespoon water

1. Preheat the oven to 350°F.

2. Place the flour, garlic salt, and cayenne in a food processor; arrange the margarine pieces on top and process until crumbs form. Add the cheese and 1 cup of the cereal; process until well blended. Transfer to a large bowl and knead until a dough forms.

3. Form the mixture, by level tablespoonfuls, into balls; flatten into ⅜-inch-thick rounds. Beat the egg white and water; dip the rounds into the egg mixture and coat on both sides with the remaining 1 cup cereal. Place on an ungreased baking sheet. Bake for 20 to 23 minutes, or until lightly browned and crisp. The wafers will become crispier after cooling. Transfer to a wire rack and cool.

Yield: 27 wafers

SHREDS

Oven-Crusted Potatoes

Remember pot roast with those sweet-tasting little red potatoes? Lately, I've been skipping the pot roast; instead, for an easy, light, but filling meal I often roast just the potatoes and eat them with a salad. Coating the potatoes in shredded wheat cereal makes them even crustier. Use either Nabisco Shredded Wheat Spoon Size, Shredded Wheat, or Shredded Wheat 'N Bran.

    2 pounds small red potatoes (1¼ to 1½ inches in diameter)
    ¼ cup olive oil
    2 cups crushed cereal
    ¼ cup grated Romano or Parmesan cheese
    2 tablespoons dried minced onion
    ½ teaspoon salt
    ½ teaspoon pepper

1. Preheat the oven to 350°F.
2. Toss the potatoes in the oil to coat well.
3. Combine the cereal, cheese, onion, salt, and pepper in a shallow dish. Dredge the potatoes in the mixture and place on a rack in a baking pan.
4. Bake for 40 to 45 minutes, or until tender and crusty.

Yield: 4 to 6 servings

THE GOOD STUFF

Pear Streusel Acorn Squash

If you've got to take a vegetable to a holiday dinner, this is the one to pick. It tastes like a combination of poached pears in amaretto and buttery acorn squash with a crunchy granola topping. Granola without fruit (raisins are added in the recipe) adds texture and sweet flavor: Quaker Sun Country Granola with Almonds, 100% Natural Granola Oats & Honey; Kellogg's Low Fat Granola without Raisins.

2 acorn squash (1¼ pounds each)
2 firm, ripe pears, peeled, seeded, and cut into ½-inch cubes
¼ cup golden raisins or finely diced dates
¼ cup plus 2 tablespoons pear nectar or apple juice
2 tablespoons amaretto liqueur or pear nectar
⅔ cup cereal
¼ cup firmly packed light brown sugar
½ teaspoon ground cinnamon
¼ teaspoon ground ginger (optional)
2 tablespoons butter or margarine, melted

1. Preheat the oven to 350°F.

2. Trim the ends of the squash; cut each squash into 4 equal rings. Remove the seeds and membrane. Arrange the rings in a jelly roll pan coated with cooking spray; arrange the pears and raisins evenly inside the squash rings. Combine the pear nectar and amaretto; pour evenly over the pear mixture. Cover with aluminum foil, and bake for 30 minutes.

3. Combine the cereal, brown sugar, cinnamon, ginger, if desired, and butter; mix well. Uncover the squash and sprinkle the cereal mixture evenly on top. Bake, uncovered, for 10 to 15 more minutes, or until the squash is tender and the topping is browned. Transfer to a serving plate with a spatula.

Yield: 8 servings

Blender Lunch Box Bran Muffins

Kellogg's All-Bran, Nabisco 100% Bran, and General Mills Fiber One will all measure the same and provide the right texture in this muffin.

> ⅓ cup milk, yogurt (any flavor), sour cream, or buttermilk
> 1 egg white
> ¾ cup cereal
> ¾ cup Bisquick
> 3 tablespoons sugar
> ½ teaspoon ground cinnamon
> ½ teaspoon vanilla extract

1. Preheat the oven to 400°F.

2. Add all of the ingredients in order to an electric blender; process until smooth. Spoon evenly into 3 muffin cups coated with cooking spray (fill the empty muffin cups with a little water to prevent scorching). Bake for 15 to 18 minutes. Eat warm.

Yield: 3 muffins

Putting Cereal on Everything ... and Everything on Cereal

Cereal Down Under

Banana Shake Cereal

Oranges and Cream Cereal

Tropical Quencher Cereal

Wow, I Could Have Had a Lemonade Cereal

Margaritaville Cereal

Cereal in the Middle of the Road

Cranberry Pineapple Crunch Casserole
Banana Cereal Split
Frozen Crackling Cappuccino Ice-Cream Dessert
Cookies and Cream Pie

It's Better on Top

Garlic Shred Croutons
All-Purpose Crunchy Topping

Hate Milk?

People who dislike milk or whose systems can't tolerate it have come up with some weird-sounding but great-tasting alternatives. Eat your cereal dry, or try drenching it with:

- coffee with nondairy creamer (optional)
- Cherry Coke
- yogurt or pudding
- chocolate syrup or other ice-cream topping
- canned cherry, peach, or other pie filling
- frozen yogurt
- pina colada or daiquiri mix
- fruit juice
- applesauce
- canned pineapple (crushed or chunks) with juice
- any flavor nondairy creamer, like amaretto or hazelnut
- instant breakfast mix, canned or powdered

CEREAL DOWN UNDER

These aren't exactly protein shakes, but they are close.

. . . Banana Shake Cereal: Peel and slice 1 banana; place in a single layer on a cookie sheet, and freeze until solid. Process the frozen banana and yogurt in a blender until smooth. Divide 1½ cups sweetened cereal (such as Kellogg's Froot Loops, Frosted Flakes, Apple Jacks; General Mills Frosted Cheerios, Trix, Berry Berry Kix; Post Banana Nut Crunch, Blueberry Morning; Ralston Foods Muesli, any flavor) between 2 tall glasses and pour the banana mixture over the cereal. For *Strawberry Shake Cereal:* Process 2 cups sliced strawberries and 1 cup vanilla ice cream or frozen yogurt in a blender until smooth; pour over the cereal as directed above. For *PBJ Shake Cereal:* Process ¼ cup milk, ¼ cup creamy peanut butter, 3 tablespoons grape jelly, and 2 cups vanilla ice cream in a blender until smooth. Divide 1½ cups Quaker Cap'n Crunch's Peanut Butter Crunch or General Mills Reese's Peanut Butter Puffs between 2 glasses, and pour the ice-cream mixture over.

. . . Oranges and Cream Cereal: Combine ½ cup chilled orange juice, ¼ cup vanilla yogurt, and sweetener or sugar to taste: pour over 1 cup General Mills Frosted Cheerios in a tumbler.

. . . Tropical Quencher Cereal: Process 1 cup diced cantaloupe, 1 cup sliced banana, ½ cup vanilla yogurt, 2 tablespoons frozen orange juice concentrate, and 1 tablespoon honey in a blender until smooth. Divide 2 cups Post Banana Nut Crunch between 2 glasses and pour the mixture over the cereal.

. . . Wow, I Could Have Had a Lemonade Cereal: Process 1 cup lemon sherbet and ½ cup lemonade in a blender until smooth. Pour over 1 cup Kellogg's Corn Pops; Post Honeycomb; General Mills Cheerios, Cocoa Puffs, or Kix in a glass.

. . . Margaritaville Cereal: Rub the cut side of a lime half around the rims of 2 margarita glasses; dip in a bowl of sugar to coat. Mix 1 cup chilled orange juice, ¼ cup chilled lime juice, and 2 tablespoons Cointreau or honey. Divide Quaker Oats Toasted Oatmeal or General Mills Oatmeal Crisp between the glasses and pour the juice mixture over the cereal.

CEREAL IN THE MIDDLE OF THE ROAD

The more layers of crunch cereal the merrier. Layered into a dessert crisp, cereal adds body and a crunchy streusel on top. Cereals like Kellogg's Cracklin' Oat Bran will stay crisp if frozen in whipped cream or ice cream.

. . . **Cranberry Pineapple Crunch Casserole:** Preheat the oven to 350°F. Combine 2 (15¼-ounce) cans drained pineapple chunks and 2 cups fresh or frozen cranberries; spread half of the fruit in a greased, deep 2-quart casserole. Combine 3 cups crushed Quaker Cinnamon Life, Life, or Oat Bran, 1½ cups firmly packed brown sugar, and 1½ teaspoons ground cinnamon; sprinkle half of the mixture over the fruit. Repeat the layers with the remaining fruit and cereal mixtures. Drizzle with melted butter; bake for 35 to 40 minutes, or until browned and bubbly. **Yield:** 6 servings.

. . . **Banana Cereal Split:** Slice 1 banana per person and place on a baking sheet. Sprinkle with brown sugar and cinnamon and broil until the sugar melts. Arrange the slices in a bowl; top with your favorite cereal (or one of my favorites: Post Waffle Crisp), then yogurt, frozen yogurt, or ice cream; chocolate sauce or maple syrup; whipped cream or topping; more cereal; and a cherry. You can use regular uncooked banana slices, too.

. . . **Frozen Crackling Cappuccino Ice-Cream Dessert:** Preheat the oven to 350°F. Crush enough Kellogg's Cracklin' Oat Bran to measure 3½ cups. Combine 2 cups of the cereal, ¼ cup firmly packed brown sugar, and cinnamon; press into the bottom of a 9-inch springform pan. Bake for 7 minutes. Let cool. Spread 3 cups softened chocolate ice cream over the crust; sprinkle with half of the remaining cereal and drizzle with ¼ cup commercial hot fudge sauce. Spoon 3 cups softened coffee ice cream on top; repeat the cereal and sauce layers. Cover and freeze until firm. **Yield:** 12 to 16 servings.

... Cookies and Cream Pie: Preheat the oven to 350°F. Crush enough Ralston Foods Cookie-Crisp to measure 4 cups. Measure out 2 cups and combine with ½ cup finely chopped dry-roasted peanuts and ¼ cup melted butter or margarine; press into the bottom and up the sides of a 9-inch deep-dish pie plate. Bake for 10 minutes; cool. Mix 1½ quarts fudge ripple ice cream and 1½ cups of the crushed cereal; spread over the crust. Drizzle with 2 tablespoons commercial hot fudge sauce and 2 tablespoons commercial hot caramel sauce; sprinkle with the remaining ½ cup cereal. Freeze until firm. To serve, heat additional fudge and caramel sauces and spoon onto the pie wedges. **Yield:** 8 servings.

Presidential Junk Food

Former President George Bush hates green vegetables and tried his best to hide the fact from the press. But the greatest cover-up of his administration may have been that he crumbles chocolate bars onto his cereal at breakfast. Yum—chocolate-covered Cheerios.

IT'S BETTER ON TOP

Cereal adds a crunchy topping to lots of foods you may not have considered:

- For salad toppings, use Quaker Crunchy Corn Bran; Ralston Foods Multi Bran Chex, Corn Chex, Double Chex; or the Mediterranean or Italian Munchies snack mix (see Index).

- Use Ralston Foods Corn Chex in taco salads instead of crushed tortilla chips.

- Instead of cookies, crumble Post Waffle Crisp; Ralston Foods Cookie-Crisp; General Mills Golden Grahams or Cinnamon Toast Crunch; or Quaker Cap'n Crunch's Peanut Butter Crunch on top of ice cream.

- Sprinkle Ralston Foods Rice Chex on top of take-out Chinese food instead of fried noodles. (Note: "Take-out" is important here—don't take along a bag of cereal to the restaurant.)

- Float Ralston Foods 100% Whole Grain Wheat Chex or Multi Bran Chex or any snack mix on tomato soup for croutons.

- Heat frozen waffles or pancakes, top with yogurt, frozen yogurt, or whipped topping, and sprinkle on Post Waffle Crisp.

. . . **Garlic Shred Croutons:** Add these to soups and salads—Nabisco Shredded Wheat, Shredded Wheat 'N Bran, or Shredded Wheat Spoon Size makes them *so* much crunchier than plain toasted croutons. Preheat the oven to 375°F. Combine 1 cup finely crushed cereal and 1 teaspoon garlic salt in a shallow dish. Cut Italian bread into 10 (1-inch-thick) slices; dip the bread in about ⅔ cup olive oil in a dish and then roll in the cereal mixture, pressing to adhere. Place on a baking sheet; bake for 10 minutes. Turn the slices and continue baking for 5 minutes, or until golden brown and crisp. Let cool; cut into cubes. Store in a zip-top plastic bag. **Yield:** 6 cups.

. . . All-Purpose Crunchy Topping: Sprinkle this topping on frozen casserole dinners after baking or on prepared stove-top dinners to spruce them up. Top a homemade casserole during the last 10 minutes of baking time. Sturdy flakes will stand up to baking: use General Mills Total Corn Flakes, Whole Grain Total; Kellogg's Toasted Corn Flakes. Preheat the oven to 350°F. Toss 2 cups cereal, ½ teaspoon seasoning salt, and 2 tablespoons melted butter or margarine on a large baking sheet to coat the flakes; spread in an even layer. Bake for 15 to 20 minutes, or until golden, stirring once. Let cool. **Yield:** 1¾ cups.

Note: You can store the topping in an airtight container for up to 2 days.

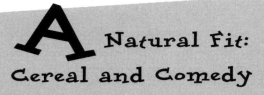

A Natural Fit: Cereal and Comedy

Bob Hope jump-starts his day with "cereal straight up, with milk." Fannie Flagg saves the best for last: "I am one of those odd ducks who like cereal at night. Just before I go to bed, nothing is better than a bowl of plain old cornflakes with sliced bananas."

Cereal's in This ?!?

Flakes

Lighter-Than-Average Crab Cakes
Special Turkey Meatballs
Savory Chili Ranch Cheesecake
Crunchy Peanut Thai Pasta
Sweet Wheaty Onion Pie
Bakery Glazed Cinnamon Raisin Biscuits

Squares

Chèvre and Wild Rice Stuffed "Porcupine" Chicken
Battered Chicken Salad

Shreds

Coconut Shrimp Almondine
Curried Walnut Wheat Burgers

The Good Stuff

Pecan Chicken Burgers
100% Natural Scalloped Apples
Maple Sweet Potato Gratin

FLAKES

Lighter-Than-Average Crab Cakes

We generally think of bread crumbs or cracker crumbs as binders in crab cakes, but think cereal crumbs instead. The following won't make the crab cakes so heavy: Post Toasties; Kellogg's Corn Flakes; General Mills Country Corn Flakes, Total Corn Flakes.

> ½ cup mayonnaise
> 1 egg, beaten
> 1 envelope Italian or Caesar salad dressing mix
> 1 pound jumbo lump crabmeat, drained
> 3 cups finely crushed cereal
> 3 tablespoons minced green onion
> 1 (2-ounce) jar chopped pimientos, drained
> 3 tablespoons butter or margarine, melted

1. Combine the mayonnaise, egg, and salad dressing mix in a large bowl; mix well. Fold in the crabmeat, ½ cup of the crushed cereal, the onion, and pimientos.

2. Using a ¼-cup measure, form the crab mixture into 2½-inch-wide, ¾-inch-thick patties. Coat with the remaining 2½ cups cereal. Transfer to a greased baking sheet. Cover and refrigerate for at least 2 hours.

3. Preheat the oven to 400°F.

4. Drizzle the crab cakes with the melted butter; bake for 15 to 20 minutes, or until browned and crisp. Serve with sour cream or tartar sauce, if desired.

Yield: about 10 crab cakes

Special Turkey Meatballs

You'll want to use milder-flavored flakes in these: Kellogg's Special K, Corn Flakes; Post Toasties; General Mills Country Corn Flakes, Total Corn Flakes.

¼ cup grated Parmesan cheese

¼ pound turkey sausage meat (remove casings)

¾ cup finely crushed cereal

2 tablespoons chopped fresh parsley

½ teaspoon crushed fennel seeds

¼ to ½ teaspoon crushed cayenne

1 cup mango chutney

⅔ cup reduced-fat sour cream

1 to 2 tablespoons dry sherry (optional)

1. Preheat the oven to 375°F.

2. Combine the cheese, sausage, cereal, parsley, fennel, and cayenne in a large bowl; mix well. Puree the chutney in a food processor or blender; measure out 2 tablespoons and add to the mixture, blending well. Form the sausage mixture into 1-inch balls. Arrange in a 15 x 10-inch jelly roll pan; bake for 25 to 30 minutes, or until the meatballs are no longer pink in the center. Drain well.

3. Pour the remaining chutney into a small saucepan; stir in the sour cream and sherry, if desired. Cook over low heat, stirring constantly, until hot. Do not boil. To serve, combine the meatballs and sauce in a small chafing dish or serving bowl.

Yield: about 40 meatballs

Savory Chili Ranch Cheesecake

These cereals make a finer, more delicate crust than bread crumbs: Kellogg's Complete Bran Flakes, Corn Flakes, Toasted Corn Flakes, Product 19, Special K; General Mills Country Corn Flakes, Whole Grain Total, Total Corn Flakes, Wheaties; Post Toasties.

1½ cups crushed cereal

1 (1-ounce) package ranch-style salad dressing mix

¼ cup butter or margarine, melted

19 ounces cream cheese, softened

2 large eggs

2½ cups (10 ounces) shredded Monterey Jack cheese with peppers

1 (4-ounce) can chopped green chilies

1 (8-ounce) carton sour cream

TOPPINGS: seeded, diced tomato; chopped green, red, or yellow
   bell pepper; sliced ripe olives; minced cilantro

1. Preheat the oven to 350°F.

2. Combine the cereal, 2 teaspoons of the salad dressing mix, and the butter in a large bowl; press into the bottom of a lightly greased 9-inch springform pan. Bake for 10 minutes. Let cool. Reduce the oven temperature to 325°F.

3. Beat the cream cheese and the remaining salad dressing mix until fluffy with an electric mixer at medium speed; add the eggs one at a time, beating after each addition. Stir in the Monterey Jack cheese and chilies.

4. Pour onto the crust; bake for 35 minutes. Remove from the oven; gently spread the sour cream on top. Let cool completely; cover and refrigerate overnight. Arrange the desired toppings over the cheesecake before serving.

Yield: one 9-inch cheesecake or 24 appetizer servings

Perfect Party Food: Savory Cheesecake

You'll get requests for this every time you're invited to a party (you may even be invited because of it). Avoid that last-minute preparty rush: you can make it up to 3 days ahead. Serve thin slices as an appetizer or larger wedges as a brunch main dish.

Crunchy Peanut Thai Pasta

I call this Thai food for meat-and-potatoes guys. Spice it up with a generous douse of hot sauce at the end. To coat the turkey, any of these cereals has the right flavor: General Mills Wheaties, Whole Grain Total, Total Corn Flakes, Country Corn Flakes; Post Toasties; Kellogg's Corn Flakes, Toasted Corn Flakes.

8 ounces spaghetti or linguine

1 large egg

2 tablespoons milk

1½ cups crushed cereal

1 pound turkey cutlets

3 tablespoons vegetable oil

3 green onions, cut into 1-inch pieces

1 large carrot, sliced thin

1 cup chicken broth

¼ cup crunchy peanut butter

1 tablespoon light teriyaki or soy sauce

1. Cook the spaghetti according to the package directions; drain and place in a large bowl.

2. Meanwhile, beat the egg and milk in a shallow dish. Place the cereal in another shallow dish or on waxed paper. Dip the turkey cutlets into the egg mixture and coat well with the cereal.

3. Heat 2 tablespoons of the oil in a large heavy skillet over medium-high heat. Add the turkey cutlets, in batches, and sauté for 3 to 4 minutes, or until browned on both sides and cooked through. Transfer to a cutting board; cut into thin strips and keep warm.

4. Heat the remaining 1 tablespoon oil in the skillet; add the onions and carrot and sauté for 3 to 4 minutes, or until the carrot is crisp-tender. Add to the drained spaghetti; toss well. Keep warm.

5. Put the chicken broth, peanut butter, and teriyaki sauce in a skillet; bring to a boil over medium heat.

6. To serve, arrange the pasta on 4 serving plates; layer on the strips of turkey, and top with the peanut sauce.

Yield: 4 servings

A Late Show Pick-Me-Up

Ever wondered how Jay Leno keeps it up night after night? Cereal with water, of course. During a show I actually saw him leave the stage, head for the water cooler, and top off a bowl of cornflakes. They admitted on national TV that he does this during every show, and proved it with cameras rolling.

Sweet Wheaty Onion Pie

The mild onion flavor of this creamy, quichelike pie is enhanced by a slightly sweet cereal crust. Use General Mills Wheaties, Whole Grain Total; Kellogg's Special K, Complete Bran Flakes, Common Sense Oat Bran; Post Bran Flakes.

1½ cups crushed cereal

¼ cup butter or margarine, melted

3 cups chopped Vidalia, Maui, Walla Walla, or Texas Sweets onion

2 tablespoons olive oil or melted butter

2 large eggs or ½ cup egg substitute

¾ cup sour cream or half-and-half

2 tablespoons minced fresh basil or thyme, or 1 teaspoon dried

½ teaspoon salt

½ teaspoon freshly ground pepper

1 cup (4 ounces) shredded Monterey Jack cheese

1. Preheat the oven to 350°F.
2. Combine the cereal and butter; mix well and press into the bottom and up the sides of a greased 9-inch pie plate.
3. Sauté the onion in the olive oil in a large heavy skillet until translucent and just tender. Pour into the crust.
4. Beat together the eggs, sour cream, basil, salt, and pepper; pour over the onions. Sprinkle with the cheese. Bake for 30 to 35 minutes, or until set.

Yield: 6 servings

Bakery Glazed
Cinnamon Raisin Biscuits

They'll think you got up early and ran to the bakery for these. Post Grape-Nuts Flakes, Bran Flakes; Kellogg's Complete Bran Flakes, Corn Flakes; or General Mills Wheaties, Whole Grain Total, Total Corn Flakes adds nutty flavor to these incredible iced biscuits.

> 1½ cups cereal
> ⅓ cup sugar
> 1 teaspoon ground cinnamon
> 2½ cups biscuit mix
> ½ cup raisins
> 1 cup plus 1 to 2 tablespoons milk
> 1 cup powdered sugar
> 2 tablespoons butter or margarine, melted

1. Preheat the oven to 400°F.

2. Combine the cereal, sugar, and cinnamon in a food processor; process until the mixture resembles fine crumbs. Transfer to a large bowl. Stir in the biscuit mix and raisins, mixing well. Add 1 cup of the milk to the mixture; stir until the dry ingredients are just moistened.

3. Turn the dough out onto a lightly floured surface and form into a ball. Pat or roll out to ¾-inch thickness. Cut out the biscuits with a 2-inch round cutter and place on a lightly greased baking sheet.

4. Bake for 15 to 18 minutes, or until golden. Transfer to a wire rack. Stir together the powdered sugar, butter, and enough of the remaining 1 to 2 tablespoons milk to make frosting of the desired consistency; spread the warm biscuits with the frosting mixture.

Yield: about 1 dozen

Chèvre and Wild Rice Stuffed "Porcupine" Chicken

Kellogg's Crispix or Ralston Foods Double Chex or Corn Chex makes a crispy coating for the chicken: a perfect wrap for the creamy herbed cheese-and-rice filling. These bundles look wonderful and taste even better.

1 (6-ounce) package long-grain and wild rice mix

8 ounces chèvre or other goat cheese

2 tablespoons minced fresh basil, thyme, or parsley

1 large garlic clove, minced

6 skinned and boned chicken breast halves

2 tablespoons dry white wine or mayonnaise

1½ cups crushed cereal

½ teaspoon pepper

1. Preheat the oven to 375°F.

2. Cook the rice according to the package directions; let cool.

3. Stir together 6 ounces of the cheese, the basil, and garlic until blended; stir in 1 cup of the cooked rice. Set aside. Place remaining rice in a small baking dish; cover and set aside.

4. Place each chicken breast half between 2 sheets of heavy-duty plastic wrap; flatten each to ¼-inch thickness using a meat mallet or rolling pin. Spoon about ¼ cup of the rice-cheese mixture onto the center of each breast half. Fold the edges to the center, overlapping one side on top. Secure with a wooden toothpick.

5. Combine the remaining 2 ounces cheese and the wine, mixing until smooth. Place the cereal and pepper on a piece of waxed paper. Coat each chicken bundle with the cheese-wine mixture and then roll in the cereal, pressing to coat. Place seam side down on a lightly greased baking sheet.

6. Bake for 25 minutes; bake the reserved rice 15 to 20 minutes, or until hot. Remove and discard the wooden toothpicks. Serve the warm chicken bundles over the heated rice.

Yield: 6 servings

The Things People Will Collect

You've heard of people collecting pottery, old books, colored glass vases, candleholders, tea sets, even picture frames. But did you know that there's a thriving collectibles market for cereal boxes?

Quake, in Chicago, Illinois, is a collectibles store specializing in cereal boxes. The owner started out with 400 Kellogg's and 600 Nabisco Shredded Wheat boxes. Prices range from $30 to $300, depending on the promotions, characters, or celebrities on the box and whether you can still buy it at the grocery store.

Battered Chicken Salad

Here's a recipe with something for everyone: if you have finicky children eating dinner, skip the greens and just give them the chicken. Quaker Crunchy Corn Bran or Toasted Oatmeal Squares adds a slightly sweet crunch.

1 garlic clove, minced

½ cup peanut oil

2 tablespoons white wine vinegar

3 tablespoons soy sauce

1 tablespoon honey

½ teaspoon freshly ground black pepper

1 pound skinned and boned chicken breast halves

1 egg white, beaten

1½ cups finely crushed cereal

4 green onions, cut into 1-inch pieces

1 red bell pepper, cut into ½-inch pieces

6 cups shredded romaine lettuce

1. Combine the garlic, ¼ cup of the oil, the vinegar, 2 tablespoons of the soy sauce, the honey, and black pepper in a jar; set aside.

2. Pound the chicken breast halves to ½-inch thickness; cut into 1-inch-wide strips. Place the chicken strips in a small bowl; toss with the remaining 1 tablespoon soy sauce, coating well. Let stand for 10 minutes; pour off the excess soy sauce. Add the beaten egg white to the chicken and toss to coat well. Roll the chicken strips one at a time in the cereal, pressing to adhere, and transfer to a plate.

3. Heat 2 tablespoons of the remaining oil in a large heavy skillet over medium-high heat. Add half of the chicken; cook for 3 to 4 minutes, or until browned and cooked through, turning the strips once. Transfer to a plate. Repeat with the remaining 2 tablespoons oil and the chicken. Add the onions and red pepper to the skillet; sauté for 2 minutes, or until crisp-tender.

4. Spoon the onions and red pepper onto the lettuce in a large bowl. Shake the salad dressing and pour over the salad; toss well. Serve immediately on 4 salad plates with the hot chicken strips arranged on top.

Yield: 4 servings

SHREDS

Coconut Shrimp Almondine

The combination of crunchy almond coating—made from Nabisco Shredded Wheat Spoon Size—with an amaretto glaze makes this dish taste decadent. Serve as an appetizer or entree.

    1 cup cereal
    ⅓ cup toasted slivered almonds
    ¼ cup flaked coconut
    ¼ teaspoon salt
    ¼ teaspoon cayenne
    1 large egg
    1 tablespoon milk
    1½ pounds large shrimp, peeled and deveined (leave tails attached)
    ½ cup all-purpose flour
    ½ cup amaretto

1. Place the cereal in a food processor and process until shredded. Add the almonds, coconut, salt, and cayenne; pulse until the almonds are finely chopped. Transfer to a shallow dish. Beat the egg and milk in a separate shallow dish.

2. Coat the shrimp one at a time with the flour, shaking off the excess. Dip the shrimp into the egg mixture and then roll in the cereal mixture, pressing to coat. Arrange on a large cooling rack placed in a jelly roll pan. (The shrimp can be prepared up to this point 2 hours ahead of cooking.)

3. Preheat the oven to 425°F.

4. Bring the amaretto to a boil in a small saucepan; boil, uncovered, until reduced to ¼ cup.

5. Bake the shrimp for 10 minutes, or until cooked. Place on a serving plate; brush lightly with the amaretto glaze.

Yield: 4 main-dish or 6 appetizer servings

Curried Walnut Wheat Burgers

These are my very favorite veggie burgers! Cereal replaces cooked grains, so they're quicker to make. Nabisco Shredded Wheat, Shredded Wheat Spoon Size, or Shredded Wheat 'N Bran holds this burger together and provides the grain flavor and texture.

2 large eggs, lightly beaten

⅓ cup plain yogurt

1 tablespoon Worcestershire sauce

2 teaspoons curry powder

½ teaspoon salt

¼ teaspoon cayenne

1 cup cooked red lentils

1 cup finely crushed cereal

½ cup finely chopped walnuts

½ cup grated carrot

½ cup minced green onion

4 sesame seed hamburger buns

CONDIMENTS: honey mustard, thinly sliced cucumber or apple, sliced red onion, alfalfa sprouts, sliced ripe olives

1. Blend the eggs, yogurt, Worcestershire sauce, curry powder, salt, and cayenne in a large bowl; mix in the lentils, cereal, walnuts, carrot, and onion. Shape into 4 (1-inch-thick) patties.

2. Place the patties on the grill on a large piece of heavy-duty aluminum foil. Cook without the grill lid over medium-high coals (350° to 400°F) 5 to 7 minutes on each side, or until done. Serve in the hamburger buns with the desired condiments.

Yield: 4 servings

Note: The patties may be broiled 4 inches from the heat source for 5 to 6 minutes on each side, or until done.

THE GOOD STUFF

Pecan Chicken Burgers

If you've ever wondered how to make moist burgers from ground chicken or turkey, adding cereal is the answer. It helps prevent the juices in naturally lean poultry from dripping out of the burgers, holding in delicious flavor. You can substitute ground turkey or lean ground pork for the chicken and easily double this recipe to serve 4. Use 1 whole, large egg instead of 2 egg yolks if you are doubling. Post Great Grains Crunchy Pecan Cereal has the perfect texture to hold the burger together, and it adds a tasty pecan accent.

1¼ cups cereal
½ pound ground chicken
¼ cup finely chopped red or green bell pepper
¼ cup finely chopped onion
1 garlic clove, crushed
1 tablespoon minced fresh thyme, basil, or dill
1 egg yolk
½ teaspoon salt
¼ teaspoon freshly ground pepper
2 hamburger buns

TOPPINGS: commercial pesto sauce, honey mustard, canned whole-berry cranberry sauce, mayonnaise, salsa

1. Crush the cereal coarsely; place ½ cup in a medium bowl and the remaining cereal in a shallow dish.

2. Add the chicken, bell pepper, onion, garlic, thyme, egg yolk, salt, and pepper to the ½ cup cereal in the bowl; mix thoroughly. Form the mixture into 2 (¾-inch-thick) patties. Coat the patties with the cereal in the shallow dish.

3. Place the patties on a large piece of heavy-duty aluminum foil and put on the grill. Cook over medium-hot coals (350° to 400°F) 5 to 6 minutes on each side, or until done. Serve in the hamburger buns with the desired toppings.

Yield: 2 servings

100% Natural Scalloped Apples

Serve as is for dessert, with whipped cream or ice cream. Or sprinkle shredded cheddar cheese on top during the last 3 minutes of baking time and serve as a side dish. Granola adds nutlike crunch to this dish. Use granolas without fruit because raisins will burn if they're baked on top: Quaker Sun Country Granola with Almonds, 100% Natural Granola Oats & Honey; Kellogg's Low Fat Granola without Raisins.

3½ cups peeled, sliced cooking apples

2 tablespoons honey

2 tablespoons apple juice or water

2 teaspoons lemon juice

¾ cup cereal

3 tablespoons light brown sugar

2 tablespoons all-purpose flour

1 tablespoon butter or margarine, melted

1. Preheat the oven to 350°F.

2. Combine the apples, honey, apple juice, and lemon juice in a large bowl; toss well. Stir in the cereal, sugar, flour, and butter; spread evenly in a greased, shallow 1-quart casserole.

3. Cover and bake for 30 minutes. Uncover and bake for 10 to 15 more minutes, or until the apples are tender and the top is crusty.

Yield: 6 to 8 servings

Maple Sweet Potato Gratin

Sweet potatoes are a Thanksgiving classic, but they are loaded with nutrients and should be on the table more often. Use cereals with fruit and nuts to add texture and sweet fruit flavor that complements the sweet potatoes: Kellogg's Just Right (any flavor), Mueslix (any flavor), Nutri-Grain (any flavor); Post Fruit & Fibre Dates, Raisins, Walnuts or Great Grains (any flavor). You can cut calories by using reduced-calorie margarine and pancake syrup. If you want to cut the dish in half for a family dinner, cook as directed below, layering in a 1-quart baking dish. Reduce the baking time to 25 minutes, covered, and 15 minutes uncovered.

> 3½ pounds sweet potatoes, peeled
> ½ cup maple-flavor pancake syrup
> ⅓ cup orange juice
> ¼ cup butter or margarine
> ¼ cup all-purpose flour
> 3 tablespoons light brown sugar
> ½ teaspoon ground cinnamon
> 1½ cups cereal

1. Cook the sweet potatoes in a large pot of boiling water for 20 to 30 minutes, or until just barely tender when tested with a fork. Drain; rinse under cold running water to stop the cooking process. Cut into ½-inch-thick slices and arrange in a greased, shallow 2-quart baking dish in concentric circles, overlapping slightly.

2. Preheat the oven to 325°F.

3. Combine the syrup and orange juice; pour over the potatoes. Cut 1 tablespoon of the butter into tiny bits and arrange evenly over the potatoes. Cover tightly with foil. Bake for 30 minutes, or until hot and the potatoes have absorbed some liquid.

4. Meanwhile, prepare the topping. Combine the flour, sugar, and cinnamon in a medium bowl. Cut in the remaining 3 tablespoons butter until the mixture resembles coarse crumbs. Stir into the cereal.

5. Sprinkle the potatoes with the topping. Bake, uncovered, for 15 to 20 more minutes, or until the topping is lightly browned and the potatoes are tender. Let stand for 10 minutes before serving.

Yield: 8 to 10 servings

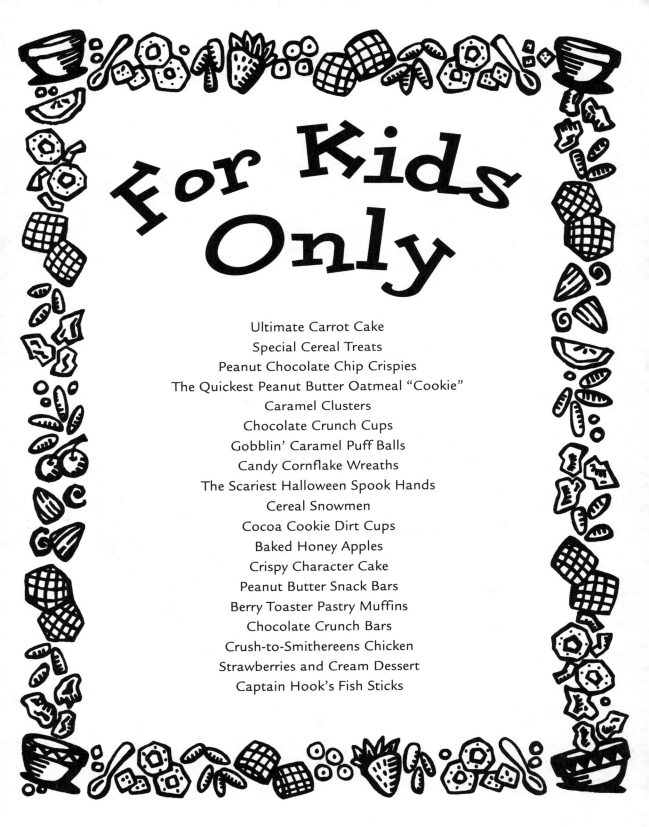

For Kids Only

Ultimate Carrot Cake

Special Cereal Treats

Peanut Chocolate Chip Crispies

The Quickest Peanut Butter Oatmeal "Cookie"

Caramel Clusters

Chocolate Crunch Cups

Gobblin' Caramel Puff Balls

Candy Cornflake Wreaths

The Scariest Halloween Spook Hands

Cereal Snowmen

Cocoa Cookie Dirt Cups

Baked Honey Apples

Crispy Character Cake

Peanut Butter Snack Bars

Berry Toaster Pastry Muffins

Chocolate Crunch Bars

Crush-to-Smithereens Chicken

Strawberries and Cream Dessert

Captain Hook's Fish Sticks

Ultimate Carrot Cake

Everybody likes carrot cake, and this one contains special cereal things that make it supermoist and supernutty. It has the bonus of extra fiber—and the extra ease of a dump-and-stir batter. Kids will love the bunny shape, which is not difficult to make. Use Post Fruit & Fibre Dates, Raisins, Walnuts or Great Grains Raisin, Date, Pecan; General Mills Basic 4; Kellogg's Just Right Fruit & Nut, Nutri-Grain Almond Raisin, Müeslix Raisin & Almond Crunch with Dates.

2 cups all-purpose or whole wheat flour

2 teaspoons baking soda

½ teaspoon salt

2 teaspoons ground cinnamon

½ teaspoon ground nutmeg

2½ cups cereal

2 cups sugar

¾ cup buttermilk

¾ cup vegetable oil

1 cup egg substitute, or 4 large eggs, lightly beaten

2 teaspoons vanilla extract

6 cups shredded carrot

1 (8-ounce) can crushed pineapple, undrained

CREAM CHEESE FROSTING

½ cup butter or margarine, softened

8 ounces reduced-fat or regular cream cheese, softened

1 (16-ounce) box powdered sugar

2 teaspoons orange rind

1 teaspoon vanilla extract

2 cups flaked coconut

Jelly beans, red licorice

1. Preheat the oven to 350°F.

2. Combine the flour, baking soda, salt, cinnamon, and nutmeg in a large bowl; stir well. Stir in the cereal. Combine the sugar, buttermilk, oil, egg

substitute, and vanilla in a large bowl; stir well with a wire whisk. Stir in the carrot and pineapple; add to the cereal mixture and stir until the dry ingredients are moistened.

3. Pour the batter into 2 greased and floured 9-inch cake pans; bake at 350°F for 30 to 35 minutes, or until a wooden toothpick inserted in the center comes out clean. Cool in the pans for 15 minutes.

4. Meanwhile, prepare the frosting. Beat the butter and cream cheese until fluffy; beat in the powdered sugar, orange rind, and vanilla.

5. Remove the cakes from the pans and let cool completely on a wire rack.

6. Cut one cake layer in half to form 2 semicircles; trim one-third off bottom of each semicircle. (Eat the trimmed portions for a snack.) Place the other cake round on a platter; arrange trimmed semicircles on edge of cake to form bunny ears. Frost with the Cream Cheese Frosting; press coconut all over the top and sides of the cake. Decorate with jelly beans for eyes, nose, and mouth and licorice for whiskers.

Yield: 1 cake

This Snack Is for the Birds

Birds love to munch, too, and they'll flock to this outdoor snacking wreath. To make it, start with a wreath—the fake, craft-store variety will last longer. Thread General Mills Cheerios—birds especially like the Honey Nut variety—or Kellogg's Froot Loops or Apple Jacks on cotton string and loop it around the wreath for garlands. Using a staple gun, attach outdoor ribbon bows to field corn that has been cut into 2- to 3-inch pieces; then tie them on the wreath. Smear bagel halves with peanut butter and press birdseed on top; tie them on the wreath, too.

Special Cereal Treats

A new taste and exciting shapes for Rice Krispies treats! Use Kellogg's Rice Krispies or Cocoa Krispies.

> **10 ounces Peppermint Patties, Andes Mints, or bite-size
> 3 Musketeers candies
> 3 tablespoons butter or margarine
> 4 cups cereal**

1. Unwrap the candies and place in a large glass bowl. Add the butter. Microwave on HIGH for 2 to 3 minutes, or until melted, stirring after 1½ minutes and then every 30 seconds. Stir in the cereal.

2. To make shapes or bars, press the mixture into an 8- or 9-inch square baking pan coated with cooking spray. Chill until firm. Cut out shapes with cookie cutters or cut into 12 bars. To make holiday egg nests, coat your hands with cooking spray and shape into 16 (3-inch) nests on a platter; let cool. Fill with jelly beans or other small candies. To make ice-cream cups, spoon the mixture evenly into 14 (2½-inch) muffin cups coated with cooking spray; coat your hands with cooking spray and press the mixture firmly to the bottom and sides of the cups. Let cool; remove from the cups and fill with ice cream or other goodies. Store these treats in the refrigerator.

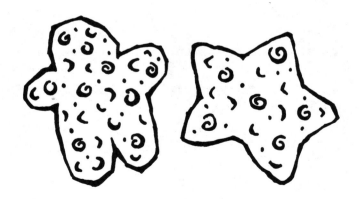

Peanut Chocolate Chip Crispies

Use Kellogg's Rice Krispie Treats Cereal for a peanut butter chocolate chip Rice Krispie Treats bar you'll make again and again. For a change of taste, substitute almond brickle chips for the peanuts and peanut butter morsels for chocolate morsels; use chunky peanut butter.

> 1 cup sugar
> 1 cup light corn syrup
> 1 cup peanut butter
> 6 cups cereal
> ¾ cup chopped peanuts
> 1 cup semisweet chocolate morsels

1. Bring the sugar and corn syrup to a boil in a heavy saucepan, stirring constantly. Remove from the heat and stir in the peanut butter until smooth.

2. Combine the cereal and peanuts in a large bowl; pour the peanut butter mixture evenly over the cereal and stir until well coated. Stir in the chocolate.

3. Press the mixture into a buttered 15 x 10 x 1-inch jelly roll pan. Let cool to room temperature and cut into 1½-inch squares.

Yield: 5 dozen

The Quickest Peanut Butter Oatmeal "Cookie"

Your kids will love making and eating these. Use Quaker Toasted Oatmeal or General Mills Oatmeal Crisp Almond.

> 1 (10-ounce) package peanut butter morsels
> 2 tablespoons butter or margarine
> 2 tablespoons peanut butter
> 3½ cups cereal
> ¼ cup strawberry jelly
> 1 cup chopped peanuts

1. Melt the peanut butter morsels, butter, and peanut butter in a large saucepan; stir in the cereal. Drop tablespoonfuls onto waxed paper; press into flat, 2-inch round cookies. Let stand until firm.

2. Stir the strawberry jelly until runny; drizzle on the cookies and sprinkle with the chopped peanuts.

Yield: 4 dozen

Caramel Clusters

This chewy candy needs a sugar-coated cereal that will stay crisp, such as Quaker Toasted Oatmeal; Kellogg's Corn Pops, Rice Krispies, Temptations French Vanilla Almond, Nut & Honey Crunch; Post Honey Bunches of Oats; General Mills Oatmeal Crisp Almond.

> 1 (14-ounce) package caramels (48 pieces), unwrapped
> ¼ cup milk or half-and-half
> 5 cups cereal

Place the caramels in a large saucepan. Add the milk; cook over low heat, stirring frequently, until the candy melts and the mixture is smooth. Remove from the heat and stir in the cereal. Drop tablespoonfuls onto waxed paper and let cool until set.

Yield: about 3 dozen

Chocolate Crunch Cups

All of a sudden, my house has been the one requested for spend-the-night parties. I think it's because I make the girls' favorite sleep-over party snacks with Kellogg's Rice Krispies or Cocoa Krispies.

> 1 (12-ounce) package chocolate morsels
> 1 (14-ounce) can low-fat or regular sweetened condensed milk
> 1¼ cups cereal

1. Melt the chocolate with the condensed milk in a large saucepan; remove from the heat, and stir in the cereal. Spoon 2 to 3 tablespoons of the mixture into paper-lined miniature muffin cups and spread on the bottom and up the sides of each cup. Or spoon ¼ to ⅓ cup of the mixture into paper-lined 2½-inch muffin cups and spread as above. Freeze or refrigerate until firm.

2. Before serving, remove the paper liners and fill the cups with candies or ice cream. Store in an airtight container in the refrigerator.

Yield: 1 to 1½ dozen

Gobblin' Caramel Puff Balls

Use General Mills Reese's Peanut Butter Puffs, Kix; Kellogg's Corn Pops, Smacks; or Post Golden Crisp instead of popcorn in these Halloween goodies. The Rice Krispies adds apple flavor and different texture; you can leave it out, however, and use 2 cups of the same cereal you chose from the above list.

> 6 cups cereal
>
> 2 cups Kellogg's Apple Cinnamon Rice Krispies or Rice Krispies
>
> ½ cup finely chopped dried apples
>
> 1 (14-ounce) package caramels (48 pieces), unwrapped
>
> 2 tablespoons water
>
> 2 tablespoons butter or margarine

1. Combine the cereals and apples in a large bowl and set aside. Cook the caramels, water, and butter in a heavy saucepan over low heat until melted, stirring frequently. Pour over the cereal mixture and toss to coat. Cool for 5 minutes.

2. Slightly dampen your hands or coat your palms with cooking spray; shape 8 balls of the mixture around the tops of wooden sticks. Place on lightly greased waxed paper. Wrap in plastic wrap to store.

Yield: 8 servings

Candy Cornflake Wreaths

Keep these great holiday treats in the refrigerator so the cereal will stay crisp. Choose from Kellogg's Corn Flakes; General Mills Country Corn Flakes, Wheaties Honey Gold, Total Corn Flakes.

> 1 (7-ounce) jar marshmallow creme
> 4 (1-ounce) squares white chocolate, chopped
> ¼ cup butter or margarine
> 1 teaspoon vanilla extract
> Green food coloring
> 3½ cups cereal
> Red hots

1. Combine the marshmallow creme, chocolate, and butter in a large saucepan; cook over medium heat, stirring constantly until melted. Remove from the heat; stir in the vanilla and tint with the food coloring. Pour over the cereal in a large bowl and stir to coat well.

2. Drop by heaping teaspoonfuls onto a baking sheet lined with waxed paper. Poke a hole in the center of each with your fingertip; add the red hots for centers. Refrigerate.

Yield: 25 wreaths

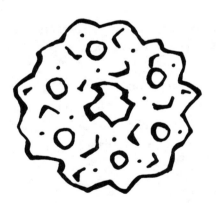

The Scariest Halloween Spook Hands

Use General Mills Cocoa Puffs to make these ideal party favors and trick-or-treat surprises. Or just have fun making these with your children.

> 3 cups cereal
> 3 cups miniature marshmallows
> 2 cups candy corn

Combine all the ingredients. Fill disposable clear plastic gloves with the mixture, pushing the mixture into the fingers to fill them, and tie at the wrists with orange and black ribbon. Add a plastic spider ring on a finger.

Primo Marketing Strategies: Toys in the Box

How in the world do you get people to buy *your* cereal and not *theirs?* You put a free prize in the box and a big neon sign on the outside that has the words "Free inside!" Cereal companies have been using premiums as a sales tool since 1910 when the first treat—The Jungleland Funny Moving Pictures Book—was packed inside a box of Kellogg's Corn Flakes. Over the years, we've found prizes of all kinds in our cereal, from metal license plates of the states to baseball cards to easily assembled miniature toys.

The king of the cereal prize enterprise is Manny Winston, a toy designer and manufacturer based in Highland Park, Illinois. He's been making the little goodies since 1958, when he was a graphic artist for Quaker Oats and was asked to create a premium toy. He invents as many as 5 toys per week, staying within the 5-cent-per-toy maximum most cereal companies are willing to spend.

Cereal Snowmen

Shaping and decorating these little guys is a fun snowy-day project for kids. General Mills Kix, Reese's Peanut Butter Puffs, Cocoa Puffs, or Trix has the best shape for molding and the biggest crunch.

> 15 cups cereal
> ½ cup butter or margarine
> 2 (10-ounce) packages miniature marshmallows
>
> **DECORATIONS:** pretzel sticks, raisins, candy corn, mini jawbreakers, gumdrops, red hots, fruit leather

1. Place the cereal in a very large bowl. Melt the butter in a heavy saucepan over medium-low heat. Add the marshmallows; cook and stir until melted. Pour over the cereal and stir to coat.

2. Slightly dampen your hands or coat your palms lightly with cooking spray. Form half of the mixture into large balls, using 1 cup mixture per ball. Form the remaining mixture into medium and small balls to stack on the snowmen bases. Stack the cereal balls to form snowmen; push pretzel-stick arms into the sides of the middle ball. Add raisins for eyes and make candy-corn noses. Arrange a row of mini jawbreakers, gumdrops, or red hots for buttons. For snowmen's scarves, cut rectangles out of fruit leather and wrap around the necks.

Yield: 6 to 7 snowmen

Tip: If your cereal balls aren't sticky enough to hold the decorations, or if the snowmen bodies won't stay stacked, mix up a small batch of stiff white icing to use as glue: place ½ cup powdered sugar in a bowl and stir in water, a few drops at a time, until a paste forms.

Cocoa Cookie Dirt Cups

Let your kids make their own dirt cups; it'll take up some time and they'll have a blast. This ultimate birthday party treat gets messy, so lay down a tarp and then send them outside to eat. Use Ralston Foods Cookie-Crisp or General Mills Cocoa Puffs or Reese's Peanut Butter Puffs for the cereal.

> 2 cups cereal
> 20 cream-filled chocolate sandwich cookies, such as Oreo Double Stuff
> 8 to 10 wafer ice-cream cones
> 8 to 10 gummy worms

Combine the cereal and cookies in a heavy zip-top plastic bag; use a rolling pin to crush until the cookies are crumbled. Spoon into the ice-cream cones; push the gummy worm candies into the dirt. If desired, arrange yellow, red, green, and blue M&Ms on top of the dirt for flowers. Serve with spoons to eat.

Yield: 8 to 10 dirt cups

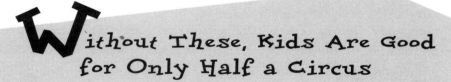

Without These, Kids Are Good for Only Half a Circus

If it's not your style to spend more money at the concession stand than on tickets for an event, bag these cereals for kids to munch on:

Quaker Popeye Cocoa Blasts, Marshmallow Stars; Kellogg's Pop-Tarts Crunch, Double Dip Crunch; General Mills Count Chocula, Cinnamon Toast Crunch, S'Mores Grahams, Reese's Peanut Butter Puffs; Post Waffle Crisp; Ralston Foods Cookie-Crisp.

Or try this mixture: 3 cups Ralston Foods Cookie-Crisp or Graham Chex, 2 cups pretzel sticks, 2 cups miniature marshmallows or peanuts, and 2 cups Snow Caps or chocolate morsels.

Baked Honey Apples

My daughter loves these for after-school snacks. The apples are tender after baking with a sweet crunchy coating. For the honey flavor, use Quaker Toasted Oatmeal Honey Nut; General Mills Honey Frosted Wheaties; Kellogg's Nut & Honey Crunch; Post Honey Bunches of Oats.

   1 cup coarsely crushed cereal
   1 large egg
   1½ tablespoons honey
   2 apples, peeled and cored

1. Preheat the oven to 350°F.
2. Place the cereal in a shallow dish. Beat the egg and honey until blended. Cut the apples into 6 wedges each; dip into the egg mixture and roll in the cereal. Place on a greased baking sheet; bake for 15 to 20 minutes, or until the apples are tender and the cereal is golden, turning once. Serve with ice cream, if desired.

Yield: 3 to 4 servings

Crispy Character Cake

Give Rice Krispies treats a new identity by making them chocolate with Kellogg's Cocoa Krispies—and in a specialty cake pan. Whether the kids are fond of dinosaurs, teddy bears, or bunny rabbits, any shape pan will hold this mixture. For easier handling, line the pan with overlapping sheets of plastic wrap. When you invert the cooled "cake" on a large platter or board, just peel off the plastic. If you signed up to bring a party treat to your child's class, this will have them congratulating your child for weeks.

Decorator candies: red or black shoestring licorice, gumdrops,
    hot cinnamon candies, small jelly beans
1 (10-ounce) package large marshmallows
¼ cup plus 2 tablespoons butter or margarine
¼ cup light corn syrup
8 ounces chocolate-flavored candy coating, chopped fine
6 cups cereal
1 cup crushed chocolate-coated peanuts or raisins
1 cup crushed chocolate-coated toffee (Heath Bars)

1. Line a teddy bear pan or other specialty cake pan with overlapping plastic wrap extending 5 inches beyond the sides of the pan. Place the decorator candies in the pan to form the character's face and body; set aside.

2. Combine the marshmallows, butter, corn syrup, and candy coating in a large saucepan; cook over low heat until smooth, stirring constantly. Remove from the heat and add the cereal, stirring until evenly coated. Stir in chocolate-coated peanuts and toffee.

3. Press the mixture evenly into the prepared pan. Fold plastic wrap over the mixture. Let stand at room temperature until cool.

Yield: 14 to 16 servings

Note: Vanilla-flavored candy coating can be substituted for chocolate-flavored. You can also use white candy-coated peanuts and raisins, almond brickle chips, and any of the following cereals: Kellogg's Apple Cinnamon Rice Krispies, Frosted Rice Krispies, Rice Krispies, or Fruity Marshmallow Krispies.

Peanut Butter Snack Bars

Nutritious cereal, such as Post Grape-Nut Flakes, Bran Flakes, Toasties, or Kellogg's Complete Bran Flakes, Common Sense Oat Bran, makes these brownielike snack cake bars good lunch-box desserts. After cooling and cutting, wrap individually or 2 by 2 in heavy-duty plastic wrap; place in a freezer bag and freeze up to 1 month. Take them out and add to lunch boxes as needed.

 ¾ cup cereal
 ½ cup self-rising flour
 1 (14-ounce) can nonfat or low-fat sweetened condensed milk
 1¼ cups peanut butter
 ½ cup butter or margarine, melted
 2 large eggs
 1 teaspoon vanilla extract
 Sifted powdered sugar

1. Preheat the oven to 350°F.
2. Combine all the ingredients except the powdered sugar in a large mixing bowl; beat with an electric mixer until blended. Spread in a greased 13 x 9 x 2-inch baking pan; bake for 25 to 30 minutes, or until a wooden toothpick inserted in the center comes out clean. Let cool in the pan on a wire rack. Sprinkle with the powdered sugar and cut into bars.

Yield: 24 bars

Berry Toaster Pastry Muffins

I'm a little reluctant to eat a toaster pastry every morning, but I'd eat these healthy muffins all day long. They're jam-filled and topped with a sweet glaze. The cereal makes a richer-tasting muffin; choose from: General Mills Wheaties Honey Gold or Healthy Choice from Kellogg's Multi-Grain Flakes.

1 cup plain yogurt

¼ cup milk

¼ cup melted margarine

1 large egg

1 teaspoon vanilla extract

1½ cups cereal

1¼ cups all-purpose flour

⅓ cup sugar

1 tablespoon baking powder

½ teaspoon baking soda

½ teaspoon salt

⅓ to ½ cup blueberry or strawberry preserves

SUGAR GLAZE

1 cup powdered sugar

2 tablespoons melted butter or margarine

1 tablespoon milk

Colored sugar sprinkles (optional)

1. Preheat the oven to 425°F.

2. Whisk the yogurt, milk, margarine, egg, and vanilla in a large bowl until blended; stir in the cereal. Let stand for 10 minutes.

3. In a separate bowl, stir together the flour, sugar, baking powder, baking soda, and salt. Add to the cereal mixture, stirring until the dry ingredients are just moistened.

4. Spoon half of the batter evenly into greased muffin tins. Place about 1 teaspoon of the preserves in the center of the batter in each muffin cup; spoon the remaining batter over the preserves. Bake for 15 to 20 minutes, or until done. Let stand for 5 minutes in the muffin tins and then transfer the muffins to wire racks.

5. To make the sugar glaze, mix the powdered sugar, butter, and milk until smooth.

6. Spoon the glaze evenly over the muffins; decorate with colored sprinkles, if desired. Serve warm or at room temperature. Refrigerate leftovers.

Yield: 1 dozen

Chocolate Crunch Bars

Move over, Nestle's Crunch Bars. This homemade version couldn't be easier to make. Try them with raisins—it's unbelievably good. Make these with Kellogg's Cocoa Krispies or Rice Krispies.

3 (2.15-ounce) Milky Way Bars, diced fine
¾ cup milk-chocolate or semisweet chocolate morsels
¼ cup plus 1 tablespoon butter or margarine
3 cups cereal
½ cup raisins or chopped peanuts

1. Line an 11 x 7-inch baking pan with aluminum foil, lightly greased.

2. Combine the diced Milky Ways, chocolate morsels, and butter in a heavy medium saucepan and cook over low heat, stirring until melted and smooth. Remove from the heat; stir in the cereal and raisins. Scrape into the prepared pan and press into an even layer with the back of a spoon.

3. Cover and refrigerate until firm. Use the foil edges to lift out of the pan. Cut into squares.

Yield: 15 squares

Crush-to-Smithereens Chicken

What child can resist the invitation to crush something to bits, whether it's a new toy or a bag of Kellogg's Crispix; Ralston Foods Corn Chex, Double Chex; or Quaker Crunchy Corn Bran? My daughter loves to help dunk the chicken into the butter and cereal mixture, and she's always especially proud of the results: a crispy taco-flavored coating on tender chicken.

> 4 cups cereal
> 1 package taco seasoning mix
> ¼ cup butter or margarine, melted
> 6 skinned and boned chicken breast halves

1. Preheat the oven to 375°F.

2. Pour the cereal into a heavy-duty plastic zip-top bag; squeeze out the air and seal. Use a rolling pin to crush the cereal into crumbs. Add the taco seasoning mix to the bag and shake to blend.

3. Transfer the crumbs into a pie plate. Pour the butter into a shallow bowl. Dip the chicken breast halves in butter one by one and then roll in the crumbs, pressing to adhere (for chicken fingers, cut the breast halves into 1½-inch strips).

4. Place in a large shallow baking pan. Mix together any leftover crumbs and butter and sprinkle over the chicken. Bake for 35 to 45 minutes, or until the chicken is done. Serve with salsa or ketchup.

Yield: 6 servings

Strawberries and Cream Dessert

For a triple dose of strawberry flavor use Kellogg's Pop-Tarts Crunch Frosted Strawberry.

1 package (3.4-ounce) instant vanilla pudding mix
2 cups milk
¼ cup strawberry-flavored Nestle's Quik
3 cups frozen whipped topping, thawed
3 cups cereal
2 cups sliced strawberries

Prepare the pudding mix according to the package directions, using the milk. Stir the Nestle's Quik into the pudding along with the milk. Let it chill for 5 minutes; fold in the whipped topping. Refrigerate 10 minutes or until serving time. Layer the mixture with the cereal and strawberries in deep bowls or large stemmed glasses. Serve immediately.

Yield: 4 servings

Double Dip Banana Pudding: Layer prepared pudding (instant or refrigerated vanilla); Post Banana Nut Crunch, General Mills Cinnamon Toast Crunch, or Kellogg's Double Dip Crunch; and sliced bananas in large stemmed glasses. Serve immediately.

Fun Facts from Kellogg

Kellogg controls 40% of the cereal market. If all Kellogg's cereal boxes made since 1906 were placed side by side, they would ring the earth 3,000 times. Put another way, if all Kellogg's cereal boxes made since 1906 were lined up end to end, they would make a round trip to the moon 160 times.

Captain Hook's Fish Sticks

The younger set will be reeled in with these don't-let-them-know-it's-healthy fish sticks. Batter them with Kellogg's Corn Flakes, General Mills Country Corn Flakes, Nabisco Team Flakes, or Post Toasties.

⅓ cup milk, buttermilk, yogurt, or reduced-fat sour cream
¼ cup reduced-fat mayonnaise
1½ cups finely crushed cereal
¾ to 1 teaspoon lemon pepper seasoning
1 pound (1-inch-thick) cod or flounder fillets, cut into 4 x 1-inch strips
Butter-flavor vegetable cooking spray

1. Preheat the oven to 450°F.

2. Combine the milk and mayonnaise in a shallow dish, mixing well. Combine the cereal and lemon pepper seasoning in a second shallow dish.

3. Dip each piece of fish into the mayonnaise mixture and then press into the cereal mixture, coating on all sides. Transfer to a jelly roll pan coated with cooking spray.

4. Bake for 12 to 15 minutes, or until the fish sticks are browned and flake easily. Serve with tartar sauce or ketchup.

Yield: 4 to 6 servings

All You Need to Know About Ninja Turtles

Here's what they won't eat on their pizza: anchovies. Big deal, you say: most *people* don't like them either. However, would you order *chocolate cereal, ice cream, and bananas* on your *pizza*? That's the Ninja Turtle Special.

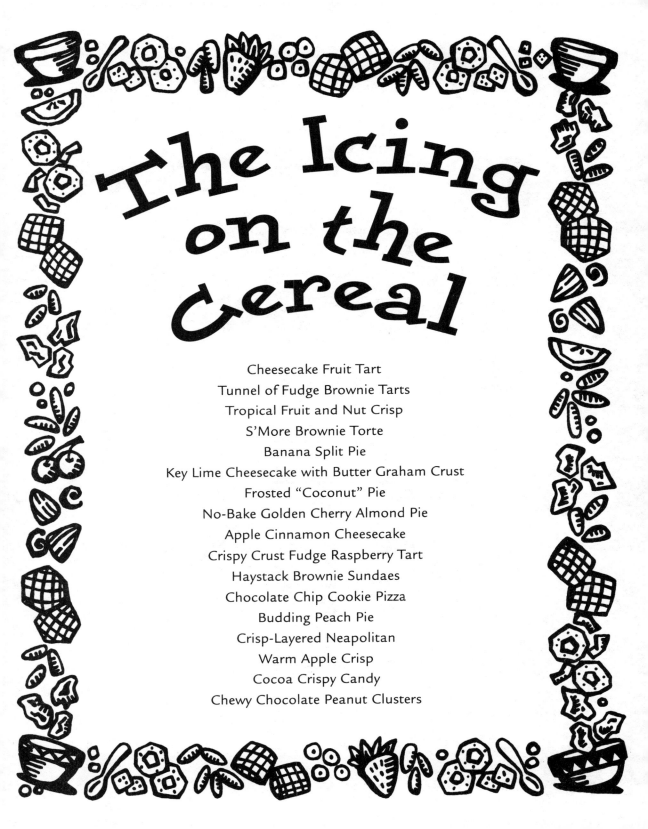

The Icing on the Cereal

Cheesecake Fruit Tart

Tunnel of Fudge Brownie Tarts

Tropical Fruit and Nut Crisp

S'More Brownie Torte

Banana Split Pie

Key Lime Cheesecake with Butter Graham Crust

Frosted "Coconut" Pie

No-Bake Golden Cherry Almond Pie

Apple Cinnamon Cheesecake

Crispy Crust Fudge Raspberry Tart

Haystack Brownie Sundaes

Chocolate Chip Cookie Pizza

Budding Peach Pie

Crisp-Layered Neapolitan

Warm Apple Crisp

Cocoa Crispy Candy

Chewy Chocolate Peanut Clusters

Mock Apple Pie
Pear Baklava Torte
Honey Almond Fruit Crumble with Sweet Lemon Cream
Fruit and Grain Zucchini Spice Cake
Better-Than-Bread Pudding
Just Right Shoofly Pie
Fruit-Filled Ice-Cream Pie
Chocolate Oatmeal Cookie Mousse Parfaits
Upside-Down Blueberry Crunch Cake
Apple Praline Oatmeal Crisp Pie
Frosty Fruit Salad with Oats and Honey

Cheesecake Fruit Tart

Use Kellogg's Pop-Tarts Crunch Frosted Brown Sugar Cinnamon or Frosted Strawberry to make a crust that reminds you of a frosted breakfast pastry. The creamy cheesecakelike filling is crowned with beautiful summer-fresh fruit.

4½ cups cereal

½ cup butter or margarine, melted

2 (3-ounce) packages cream cheese, softened

½ cup ricotta or cottage cheese

⅓ cup powdered sugar

1 teaspoon vanilla extract

2 cups frozen whipped topping, thawed

3 cups fresh or thawed frozen fruit: blueberries, strawberries,
   sliced peaches, sliced kiwi, sliced banana, raspberries

2 tablespoons apple jelly or strawberry jam, melted

1. Combine the cereal and butter in a food processor and process until crushed and blended. Press the mixture onto the bottom and up the sides of a 9-inch tart pan or pie plate. Chill 1 hour, or until firm.

2. Combine the cream cheese, ricotta, powdered sugar, and vanilla in the food processor; process until smooth.

3. Transfer to a large bowl and fold in the whipped topping. Spread evenly in the piecrust. Arrange the fruit attractively on top of the filling; brush with the apple jelly. Refrigerate for 4 hours, or until well chilled.

Yield: one 9-inch pie

Tunnel of Fudge Brownie Tarts

Make sure you crush the cereal to a fine powder to make these brownie cups moist and dense, perfect for holding the creamy chocolate filling. Choose from General Mills Honey Nut Cheerios, Multi-Grain Cheerios; Kellogg's Nut & Honey Crunch O's.

> 1½ cups cereal
> ⅔ cup plus 1½ tablespoons all-purpose flour
> ½ cup butter or margarine, cut into pieces and softened, plus
>   2 tablespoons butter or margarine
> 1 (3-ounce) package cream cheese, cut into pieces and softened
> 2 (1-ounce) squares unsweetened chocolate
> ¼ cup plus 3 tablespoons sugar
> 1 large egg
> ½ teaspoon vanilla extract

1. Preheat the oven to 400°F.

2. Place the cereal in a food processor and process until finely crushed. Add ⅔ cup of the flour and pulse until blended. Arrange the ½ cup butter and the cream cheese pieces on the dry ingredients; pulse until the mixture forms a dough. Wrap in plastic wrap and press into a disk; refrigerate for 2 hours.

3. Microwave the chocolate and the 2 tablespoons butter in a medium bowl on HIGH for 45 seconds; stir until smooth. Stir in the sugar, the remaining 1½ tablespoons flour, the egg, and vanilla until blended. Shape the dough into 1½-inch balls; press into the bottom and up the sides of ungreased miniature muffin cups. Bake for 8 minutes, or until very lightly browned. Remove from the oven; reduce the oven temperature to 325°F.

4. Spoon the chocolate mixture evenly into the muffin cups. Bake for 18 to 20 more minutes, or until the filling is set. Cool in the pans for 10 minutes; remove from the pans and let cool completely on wire racks.

Yield: 22 tarts

Tropical Fruit and Nut Crisp

Top with vanilla yogurt for brunch, or frozen yogurt or ice cream for dessert. The decadent taste comes from Post Banana Nut Crunch; Kellogg's Temptations French Vanilla Almond or Temptations Honey Roasted Pecan.

1 (8-ounce) can pineapple chunks in unsweetened juice, undrained
1 teaspoon quick-cooking tapioca, or 2 teaspoons cornstarch
1 banana, sliced
2 cups sliced fresh or thawed frozen peaches
¼ cup firmly packed brown sugar
2 tablespoons all-purpose flour
¼ cup butter or margarine, cut into bits
1½ cups cereal

1. Preheat the oven to 375°F.
2. Combine the pineapple and tapioca in a 2-quart baking dish, stirring well. Mix in the banana and peaches.
3. In a separate bowl, combine the brown sugar, flour, and butter, mixing until crumbly. Mix in the cereal. Sprinkle evenly over the fruit.
4. Bake for 20 to 25 minutes, or until the topping is lightly browned and the fruit is bubbly. Serve warm.

Yield: 4 to 6 servings

S'More Brownie Torte

To make a light version, use a 20-ounce package of light brownie mix and low-fat frozen yogurt. General Mills Golden Grahams or Ralston Foods Graham Chex makes the graham layer in this yummy ice-cream sandwich bar.

> 1 (21.5-ounce) package fudge brownie mix
> 2 pints frozen vanilla or chocolate yogurt, softened
> 2 cups coarsely crushed cereal
> Chocolate sauce (optional)

1. Preheat the oven to 350°F.

2. Prepare the brownie mix according to the package directions using a 13 x 9 x 2-inch baking pan. Bake for 18 to 20 minutes; let cool to room temperature on a wire rack.

3. Spread the yogurt over the cooled brownies. Sprinkle the crushed cereal over the yogurt; press lightly into the yogurt. Cover and freeze until solid. Cut into bars; top with chocolate sauce, if desired.

Yield: 16 servings

Cheering Cheerios

- Cheerios were called Cheerioats when they were first marketed in 1941. The name was changed in 1945 because they looked more like Os than oats.
- If you were to line up Cheerios side by side around the equator, it would take 3,155,524,416 of them. You'd be pretty toasty yourself by then.

Banana Split Pie

You'd better make more than one, because this will disappear fast. It's the perfect dessert to take to the Fourth of July block party. The crunchy crust holds a layered pie that tastes like a banana split. Kellogg's Cracklin' Oat Bran is the one cereal that will stay crunchy no matter what.

2 cups finely crushed cereal, plus additional for sprinkling

¼ cup butter or margarine, melted

¼ cup butter or margarine, softened

3 tablespoons whipping cream

2 cups powdered sugar

2 teaspoons vanilla extract

1 banana

1 (8-ounce) can pineapple tidbits, well drained

1½ cups thawed frozen whipped topping

½ cup chopped pecans

½ cup quartered drained maraschino cherries

1. Combine the crushed cereal and melted butter; press into the bottom and up the sides of a 9-inch pie plate. Chill 1 hour, or until firm.

2. Beat the softened butter until creamy; beat in the whipping cream, powdered sugar, and vanilla until smooth. Spread in the piecrust. Slice the banana; chop the pineapple and pat dry with paper towels. Arrange on top of the creamed mixture and press down firmly. Spread the whipped topping over the pie; sprinkle with the pecans and cherries. Refrigerate for 3 hours; sprinkle with additional cereal. Store in the refrigerator.

Yield: one 9-inch pie

Key Lime Cheesecake with Butter Graham Crust

To make it fancier, garnish with slices of papaya, mango, or kiwi. Quaker OH's—Honey Graham; General Mills Golden Grahams, Honey Nut Cheerios; or Kellogg's Nut & Honey Crunch O's makes a uniquely flavored crust, containing a filling that tastes like Key lime pie and has the consistency of cheesecake.

3 cups cereal

½ cup flaked coconut, toasted, plus additional for garnish

½ cup butter or margarine, melted

1 (8-ounce) package light or regular cream cheese, softened

1 (14-ounce) can low-fat or regular sweetened condensed milk

⅓ cup lime juice

2 cups sweetened whipped cream or thawed frozen nondairy
    whipped topping, plus additional for garnish

1. Place the cereal in a food processor and process until crushed. Add the coconut; pour the butter evenly over the mixture. Pulse until just blended. Press firmly into the bottom and up the sides of a 9-inch pie plate. Chill 1 hour, or until firm.

2. Beat the cream cheese until fluffy in a large mixing bowl; gradually beat in the condensed milk and lime juice until smooth. Fold in the whipped cream; smooth into the prepared crust. Chill for 4 hours, or until set. Garnish with additional coconut and whipped topping.

Yield: one 9-inch pie

Note: To toast coconut, spread out in a thin layer on a baking sheet; bake at 350°F for 10 to 15 minutes, or until lightly browned, stirring once.

Frosted "Coconut" Pie

Prepare this mock coconut pie with Nabisco Frosted Wheat Bites if you want to skip the cholesterol that coconut carries with it, or if somebody you're making it for won't eat coconut but loves cereal. The pudding filling is light and creamy, and the cereal baked on the crust makes the piecrust feel like a cookie in your mouth. You can substitute 1½ cups thawed frozen whipped topping for the whipped cream and powdered sugar.

1 frozen deep-dish 9-inch piecrust, thawed

2 cups cereal, crushed

1 (4-serving-size) coconut or vanilla pudding mix

1¾ cups milk

3 tablespoons coconut liqueur, rum, or milk

¾ cup whipping cream

⅓ cup sifted powdered sugar

1. Preheat the oven to 400°F.

2. Fit the piecrust into a 9-inch pie plate; prick all over with a fork. Sprinkle ¼ cup of the cereal on the bottom of the piecrust and press into the crust. Bake for 12 to 15 minutes, or until browned. If the crust puffs up, press it back against the pie plate during baking. Let cool.

3. Prepare the pudding mix according to the package directions for a pie filling using the milk and coconut liqueur; pour into the piecrust. Cover the filling with waxed paper; let cool for 30 minutes; sprinkle with an additional ½ cup cereal. Cover and chill 1 hour or until firm.

4. Beat the whipping cream until foamy; gradually add the sugar, beating until soft peaks form. Spread the whipped cream over the cereal. Sprinkle with the remaining 1¼ cups cereal.

Yield: one 9-inch pie

No-Bake Golden Cherry Almond Pie

Make the "graham cracker" crust with Ralston Foods Graham Chex, General Mills Golden Grahams, or Quaker OH's—Honey Graham.

2 cups crushed cereal
3 tablespoons brown sugar
¼ cup butter or margarine, melted
1 (14-ounce) can sweetened condensed milk
⅓ cup lemon juice
⅓ cup toasted slivered almonds, chopped, plus additional for garnish
1 (21-ounce) can cherry pie filling
1 (4-ounce) container frozen whipped topping, thawed

1. Combine the cereal, sugar, and butter in a medium-size bowl; press into the bottom and up the sides of a 9-inch pie plate. Chill 1 hour, or until firm.

2. Blend the condensed milk and lemon juice by hand in a medium bowl; stir in the almonds and 1 cup of the cherry pie filling. Fold in the whipped topping; pour evenly into the piecrust. Chill for 4 hours, or until set.

3. To serve, cut into wedges; spoon the remaining pie filling over the slices and sprinkle with additional almonds, if desired.

Yield: one 9-inch pie

Apple Cinnamon Cheesecake

Use General Mills Apple Cinnamon Cheerios or Kellogg's Apple Cinnamon Squares for a crust that matches the apple-pie flavor of this cheesecake.

2½ cups cereal

1¼ cups plus 2 tablespoons sugar

⅓ cup butter or margarine, melted

4 (8-ounce) packages light or regular cream cheese, softened

¼ cup all-purpose flour

2 teaspoons apple pie spice

3 large eggs

¼ cup frozen apple juice concentrate, thawed

1. Preheat the oven to 350°F.

2. Combine the cereal and 2 tablespoons of the sugar in a food processor and process until finely crushed. Add the butter and process until blended. Press into the bottom of a 9-inch springform pan coated with cooking spray. Bake for 10 minutes. Let cool. Reduce oven temperature to 300°F.

3. In a large mixing bowl, beat the cream cheese with an electric mixer on medium speed until fluffy. Beat in the remaining 1¼ cups sugar, the flour, and apple pie spice at low speed just until smooth. Add the eggs, one at a time, beating after each addition just until blended. Stir in the apple juice concentrate. Pour into the crust.

4. Bake at 300°F for 1 hour, or until the edges are firm but the center jiggles slightly. Turn off the oven and leave the cheesecake in the oven for 30 minutes. Remove and let cool completely on a wire rack. Cover and refrigerate overnight.

Yield: one 9-inch cheesecake

Crispy Crust Fudge Raspberry Tart

If making Cupid's finest chocolate treat for your sweetie won't get you what you want for Valentine's Day, I give up. The rich, trufflelike filling tastes as if it's made from the finest chocolates—a wonderful complement to the chocolate pastry crust made crisp with cereal. For the best crust use Kellogg's Rice Krispies or Cocoa Krispies. If fresh raspberries are hard to find or too expensive, top this tart with strawberry slices, blueberries, peaches, or any other fruit in season. It's delicious with mango: for added flair, puree 1 or 2 mangoes with 2 tablespoons brandy or amaretto and serve atop slices of the tart.

2 cups cereal

¾ cup all-purpose flour

⅓ cup sugar

3 tablespoons unsweetened cocoa powder

¼ teaspoon salt

¼ cup plus 2 tablespoons chilled butter or margarine, cut into pieces

1 egg yolk

1 cup plus 2½ to 3 tablespoons whipping cream

¼ cup plus 2 tablespoons raspberry or strawberry jam

4 ounces bittersweet or semisweet chocolate, chopped fine

Fresh raspberries

1. Preheat the oven to 375°F.

2. Place the cereal in a food processor and process until crushed. Add the flour, sugar, cocoa powder, and salt; process until blended. Sprinkle the butter pieces over the flour mixture; pulse until crumbly. Beat together the egg yolk and 2½ to 3 tablespoons of the whipping cream; drizzle over the flour mixture and process until the dough holds together. Turn the dough out onto a piece of plastic wrap and pat into a disk. Chill for 20 minutes.

3. Press the dough into the bottom and up the sides of a greased 9- to 10-inch tart pan with a removable bottom. Prick the crust with a fork; bake for 20 to 25 minutes, or until the crust is lightly browned at the edges. If the crust puffs up during baking, gently press it into the bottom and sides of the pan with the back of a spoon. Spread the jam on the bottom of the crust and bake for 2 more minutes. Let cool completely.

4. Bring the remaining 1 cup whipping cream to a boil in a heavy small saucepan; remove from the heat and add the chocolate. Whisk until smooth. Transfer to a bowl and refrigerate until chilled but not firm, about 30 to 45 minutes.

5. Using an electric mixer, beat the chocolate mixture until very thick and almost firm. Spread over the jam in the crust. Arrange the raspberries on top and sift on powdered sugar, if desired.

Yield: one 9-inch tart

Haystack Brownie Sundaes

Shredded wheat cereals make the bottom brownie layer moist on the inside and add crispy texture to the scoops of ice cream on top. Use either Kellogg's Frosted Mini-Wheats, Kellogg's Frosted Mini-Wheats Bite Size, or Nabisco Frosted Wheat Bites.

¼ cup butter or margarine
1 cup semisweet chocolate morsels
¾ cup sugar
½ cup all-purpose flour
½ teaspoon baking powder
¼ teaspoon salt
2 large eggs, lightly beaten
1 teaspoon vanilla extract
2 cups crushed cereal
Ice cream
Commercial hot fudge sauce

1. Preheat the oven to 350°F.

2. Melt the butter and chocolate in a large heavy saucepan over low heat, stirring constantly. Remove from the heat.

3. Add the sugar, flour, baking powder, salt, eggs, and vanilla; stir until well blended. Stir in 1 cup of the cereal. Spread evenly in a greased 8-inch square baking pan.

4. Bake for 30 minutes, or until the center is set. Cool in the pan on a wire rack. Cut into squares and place on serving plates. Top with scoops of ice cream and sprinkle with the remaining 1 cup of cereal. Drizzle with hot fudge sauce. Serve immediately.

Yield: 9 servings

Chocolate Chip Cookie Pizza

This is a huge cookie topped with a thin layer of sweetened cream cheese and fruit. Mixing Kellogg's Rice Krispies into the commercial cookie dough turns the usually soft cookie into a crispy "pizza" crust.

1 (18-ounce) package refrigerated chocolate chip cookie dough,
    at room temperature
2 cups cereal
3 (3-ounce) packages cream cheese, softened
¼ cup sour cream
1 large egg, beaten
2 tablespoons sugar
Fresh fruit

1. Preheat the oven to 375°F.

2. Thoroughly mix the cookie dough and cereal; press into a greased 12-inch pizza pan or a 13 x 9 x 2-inch baking pan. Bake for 5 minutes, or until just firm.

3. Blend the cream cheese, sour cream, egg, and sugar; spread on the crust. Bake for 15 to 25 more minutes, or until set. Let cool; arrange the fresh fruit on top.

Yield: 12 servings

Budding Peach Pie

This is my favorite old-fashioned peach pie. I love the streusel topping, and crystallized ginger makes the taste truly unique. The best part of this pie may be the crust: flaky, low in fat, full of fiber. Post Grape-Nuts or Kellogg's Bran Buds takes over for nuts in the crust and crumb topping. If fresh peaches are not available, substitute 2 (16-ounce) bags frozen, sliced peaches, thawed and well drained.

1¾ cups plus ⅓ cup all-purpose flour

¾ cup cereal

¼ cup plus ⅓ cup and 2 teaspoons sugar

½ teaspoon salt

½ cup margarine, melted and cooled

3 tablespoons vanilla-flavored low-fat yogurt

6 cups peeled, thinly sliced peaches

3 tablespoons minced crystallized ginger (optional)

½ teaspoon ground cinnamon

1. Preheat the oven to 425°F.

2. Combine 1½ cups of the flour, ¼ cup of the cereal, 2 teaspoons of the sugar, and the salt in a medium bowl; mix well. Stir together ¼ cup of the margarine and the yogurt. Drizzle over the flour mixture; toss with a fork until crumbly. Form into a ball.

3. Roll out the pastry ball between two sheets of plastic wrap into a 10½-inch circle and fit into a 9-inch pie plate coated with cooking spray. Trim and crimp the sides; refrigerate for 30 minutes. Prick all over with a fork and then bake for 10 to 15 minutes, or until the crust begins to color. Set aside. Reduce oven temperature to 375°F.

4. Combine the peaches, ginger, if desired, ¼ cup of the remaining sugar, and ¼ cup of the remaining flour; toss until the fruit is coated with the sugar mixture. Spoon into the pastry shell; cover the edges of the pastry with aluminum foil.

5. Combine the remaining ⅓ cup flour, the remaining ½ cup cereal, the remaining ⅓ cup sugar, and the cinnamon; mix in the remaining ¼ cup margarine until crumbly. Sprinkle over the pie; bake for 25 minutes. Remove the foil and bake for another 25 to 30 minutes, or until the top is golden and the fruit is tender.

Yield: one 9-inch pie

How Can a Bod Like That Get Depressed?

Well, it happens. And when it does, Jamie Lee Curtis professes to indulge in a big bowl of granola or shredded wheat with nonfat milk. If that is weakness, no wonder she looks the way she does.

Crisp-Layered Neapolitan

Kellogg's Cracklin' Oat Bran is THE cereal that stays crunchy in the frozen cream layer that forms the base for this summer-perfect ice-cream dessert. Serve it with hot fudge sauce and fresh strawberries.

        2 cups whipping cream
        ½ cup powdered sugar
        1 teaspoon vanilla extract
        3½ cups crushed cereal
        1 pint chocolate ice cream, softened
        1 pint strawberry ice cream, softened
        1 pint vanilla ice cream, softened

1. Beat the whipping cream in a large mixing bowl until frothy; add the powdered sugar and vanilla and beat with an electric mixer on medium speed until soft peaks form. Fold in 3 cups of the cereal.

2. Spread the cream mixture in a 9-inch springform pan; freeze. Layer the ice creams over the cream mixture, allowing each layer to refreeze before spreading the next layer. Sprinkle with the remaining ½ cup cereal. Cover and freeze. Remove the side of the pan before cutting into wedges.

Yield: 12 servings

Warm Apple Crisp

This is a design-your-own-dessert recipe. Pick any of the following cereals; the result is out of this world: Ralston Foods Almond Delight; Kellogg's Temptations French Vanilla Almond or Temptations Honey Roasted Pecan, Nut & Honey Crunch; Quaker Toasted Oatmeal with Almonds or Toasted Oatmeal Honey Nut; General Mills Oatmeal Crisp Almond, Clusters, Sun Crunchers; Post Honey Bunches of Oats, Honey Bunches of Oats with Almonds.

  2 cups cereal
  1 cup firmly packed light brown sugar
  ⅓ cup all-purpose flour
  1 teaspoon ground cinnamon
  ¼ cup butter or margarine, melted
  4 medium Granny Smith apples, peeled, cored,
      and cut into ½-inch slices
  ½ cup apple juice
  ½ cup chopped pecans, toasted sliced almonds, or raisins

1. Preheat the oven to 350°F.

2. Combine the cereal, brown sugar, flour, and cinnamon in a medium-size bowl; stir well. Add the butter and stir until combined.

3. Toss 1½ cups of the mixture with the apples, reserving the remaining cereal mixture. Spoon the apple mixture into a greased 9-inch square baking pan; drizzle the juice over the apple mixture. Cover with foil, and bake for 30 minutes.

4. Add the pecans to the remaining cereal mixture and sprinkle over the apple mixture. Bake, uncovered, for 20 more minutes, or until the apples are tender and the topping is browned. Serve warm with ice cream, if desired.

Yield: 6 servings

Cocoa Crispy Candy

These taste like Reese's Peanut Butter Cups with chocolate crispies in them. If you've got to have them now, skip the chocolate coating. They'll firm up in the refrigerator in about 5 minutes. Kellogg's Cocoa Krispies makes them extra chocolaty.

3¾ cups powdered sugar
½ cup butter or margarine, softened
2 cups peanut butter
3 cups cereal
6 ounces German sweet baking chocolate, chopped
6 ounces semisweet chocolate morsels

1. In a large bowl, beat the powdered sugar, butter, and peanut butter with an electric mixer on low speed. Stir in the cereal. Roll into 1-inch balls; place on a baking sheet and refrigerate 1 hour, or until cold.

2. Melt the chocolate in a heavy saucepan over low heat, stirring frequently. (Or place the chocolate in a large glass bowl; microwave for 2 minutes on HIGH and stir until smooth.) Insert a wooden toothpick into each candy ball and dip it into the chocolate, coating the ball thoroughly and allowing the excess to drip back into the bowl. Place on a baking sheet lined with waxed paper and chill. (Don't leave the toothpicks in the balls.) Store in an airtight container in the refrigerator.

Yield: 5 dozen

Chewy Chocolate Peanut Clusters

Creamy peanut butter and chocolate—flavored candy made quick, easy, and crunchy with Quaker Oats Cap'n Crunch's Peanut Butter Crunch, Cap'n Crunch; Kellogg's Smacks, Corn Pops; Post Golden Crisp.

1 (12-ounce) package peanut butter morsels
1 (12-ounce) package semisweet chocolate or milk-chocolate morsels
¼ cup peanut butter
3 cups cereal
1 (3-ounce) can chow mein noodles
1 cup peanuts

1. Melt the peanut butter morsels, chocolate, and peanut butter in a heavy saucepan over low heat, stirring frequently.
2. Combine the cereal, chow mein noodles, and peanuts in a large bowl; pour the chocolate mixture over and stir to coat well. Drop by rounded teaspoonfuls onto waxed paper; chill 1 hour, or until firm. Store in an airtight container in the refrigerator.

Yield: about 8 dozen

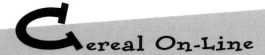

Cereal On-Line

"I was denied sweetened cereals as a child. So they became something of a fetish—all those brazenly labelled boxes of Cap'n Crunch, Froot Loops and Cocoa Krispies at the grocery store, tantalizingly within reach and yet verboten. I fantasized about buying a box at the Circle K, hiding it in my bedroom closet, and sneaking morsels of Frankenberry with the radio blasting to mask the telltale crunch. I never worked up the nerve, though."

—JC Herz (**author of** *Joystick Nation*)

Mock Apple Pie

This is a takeoff on the mock apple pie so ingeniously born of suburban cooking in the 1930s. As a substitute for the Ritz crackers used in the original, these cereals crush up sweeter and give the pie better flavor: Kellogg's Corn Pops; General Mills Kix; Quaker Oats Popeye Jeepers Crispy Corn Puffs, Cap'n Crunch. Although you'll mess up a few appliances and bowls, you can eat this pie in 30 minutes and it is absolutely delicious leftover and cold.

> 1 frozen deep-dish 9- or 9½-inch piecrust
> 2½ cups cereal
> 3 egg whites
> 1 teaspoon baking powder
> 1 teaspoon vanilla extract
> 1 cup sugar
> ½ cup pecan pieces
> 3 ounces finely chopped milk-chocolate or semisweet chocolate
>   mini morsels

1. Bake the piecrust according to the package directions. Reduce oven temperature to 350°F.

2. Process the cereal in a food processor until finely crushed; set aside. In a medium bowl, beat the egg whites, baking powder, and vanilla until foamy; gradually add the sugar, beating until soft peaks form. Fold in the cereal mixture in 2 batches; fold in the pecans and chocolate. Spoon into the piecrust.

3. Bake at 350°F for 30 minutes. Let cool. Serve warm or at room temperature with whipped cream.

Yield: one 9-inch pie

Oops! I Forgot to Make Dessert

I went to a dinner party where the host did *just that*. So, after everyone had eaten the gourmet pizzas she had prepared, she pulled cereals out of the pantry and put them on the table for the guests to help themselves. Her reasoning? "It's just like eating cookies, anyway." Some cereals are shaped for snacking, like Ralston Foods Cookie-Crisp and Post Waffle Crisp. Pour flakes like Ralston Foods Almond Delight onto small plates, so your guests won't have to root around in the box. But beware: picking sugary crunchies out of a plate of Kellogg's Temptations French Vanilla Almond is as tempting as digging the cashews out of mixed nuts.

Dessert Cereals:

Ralston Foods Almond Delight
Ralston Foods Cookie-Crisp
Post Banana Nut Crunch
Post Blueberry Morning
Post Waffle Crisp
Kellogg's Temptations French Vanilla Almond
    or Honey Roasted Pecan
Kellogg's Cracklin' Oat Bran
Kellogg's Pop-Tarts Crunch
General Mills Golden Grahams

Pear Baklava Torte

This layered pastry-pear dessert is inspired by the Mediterranean delight made by stacking phyllo dough and a honey-laden ground nut mixture. Instead of nuts, Kellogg's Frosted Mini-Wheats keeps these pastry layers crisp. You'll need 2 to 4 large cookie sheets to bake the pastry layers. If you're short on time, spend it making the torte layers, then use 2 cans apple pie filling, heated, or 2 (12-ounce) packages Stouffer's Escalloped Apples, cooked, instead of the homemade filling.

1 cup cereal
¼ cup plus 3 tablespoons sugar
1½ teaspoons ground cinnamon
16 sheets phyllo dough
⅓ cup plus 2 tablespoons butter or margarine, melted
6 cups firm, ripe pear slices, cut ¼ inch thick (about 2 pounds)
½ cup pear nectar or apple juice
½ cup hot caramel ice-cream topping
1 tablespoon brandy (optional)
Sifted powdered sugar

1. Preheat the oven to 375°F.

2. Combine the cereal, ¼ cup of the sugar, and ½ teaspoon of the cinnamon in a food processor. Process until finely shredded.

3. Stack 16 phyllo sheets on a cutting surface. Starting at one corner of the phyllo stack, use an 8-inch round cake pan as a guide to cut out a stack of circles. Repeat at the opposite corner, making a total of 32 circles. Discard the trimmings. To prevent drying, keep the circles covered with a damp cloth when not working with them.

4. Place 1 phyllo circle at the corner of a greased cookie sheet; brush lightly using ⅓ cup of the melted butter. Place another phyllo circle on top; brush with butter and sprinkle with 2 teaspoons of the cereal mixture. Repeat the layering procedure with 6 more phyllo circles, the melted butter, and cereal mixture to make 8 layers of phyllo, sprinkling the cereal mixture on every other circle. Assemble 3 additional stacks of 8 phyllo circles each on greased cookie sheets.

5. Bake for 10 minutes, or until golden and crisp. Let cool on a wire rack. To make the pear filling, place the remaining 2 tablespoons butter in a large heavy skillet over medium-high heat. Add the pears, the remaining 3 tablespoons sugar, and the remaining 1 teaspoon cinnamon. Cook and stir until the pears begin to soften. Add the pear nectar and bring to a boil. Reduce the heat and simmer, uncovered, until the liquid is nearly evaporated.

6. In a separate bowl, combine the caramel topping and brandy, if desired.

7. To assemble, place 1 stack of the phyllo on a platter. Top with one-third of the pear filling and drizzle with one-third of the caramel sauce. Continue layering with 2 more phyllo stacks and the remainder of the filling and sauce. End with a phyllo stack layer. Sprinkle with sifted powdered sugar and serve immediately.

Yield: 6 servings

Honey Almond Fruit Crumble with Sweet Lemon Cream

Spotlight these beautiful summer fruits and berries in a light dessert with a nutritious topping made from Ralston Foods Almond Delight, Quaker Toasted Oatmeal Honey Nut, General Mills Oatmeal Crisp Almond, or Post Honey Bunches of Oats with Almonds. You can substitute 1 (16-ounce) bag frozen sliced peaches, thawed and drained, for fresh peaches. Turn it into a brunch dish by adding Sweet Lemon Cream and serving with an omelet or frittata and a loaf of crusty bread.

3 cups halved fresh strawberries

1 cup fresh blueberries or raspberries

6 fresh peaches or large plums, peeled, seeded, and sliced

⅓ cup sugar

2 tablespoons quick-cooking tapioca

2 teaspoons lemon juice

1 teaspoon ground cinnamon

TOPPING

½ cup all-purpose flour

⅔ cup firmly packed light brown sugar

1 teaspoon ground cinnamon

1 teaspoon ground ginger

½ teaspoon ground allspice

¼ cup plus 2 tablespoons butter or margarine

1½ cups cereal

SWEET LEMON CREAM

1 (8-ounce) container vanilla yogurt

2 tablespoons honey

2 teaspoons lemon juice

1. Combine the strawberries, blueberries, peaches, sugar, tapioca, lemon juice, and cinnamon in a bowl; cover and let stand at room temperature for 1 to 3 hours.

2. Meanwhile, make the topping. Combine the flour, brown sugar, cinnamon, ginger, and allspice in a large bowl; cut in the butter until the mixture resembles coarse meal. Or combine in a food processor and pulse until the mixture forms coarse crumbs. Stir in the cereal.

3. Preheat the oven to 375°F.

4. Transfer the fruit filling to a greased 12 x 8 x 2-inch glass baking dish. Sprinkle the topping over the filling, covering completely. Bake for 40 minutes, or until the fruit is bubbly and the topping is lightly browned.

5. To make the Sweet Lemon Cream, stir together the yogurt, honey, and lemon juice.

6. Serve warm with Sweet Lemon Cream or frozen yogurt.

Yield: 6 to 8 servings

Fruit and Grain Zucchini Spice Cake

This layer cake is packed with good-for-you ingredients and even starts from a low-fat cake mix. It's the kind of dessert you'd make to surprise your family because baking a cake is not often done. But this one is easy, and you'll love the flavor of the fat-free frosting. If you're short on time, stir the spices into a can of reduced-fat vanilla frosting and spread away. Reduced-fat cake mixes are sometimes too fluffy and airy, so to make the cake richer in texture and flavor add one of these cereals: Kellogg's Müeslix Crispy Blend, Mueslix Golden Crunch, or Nutri-Grain Golden Wheat.

    1 (18.5-ounce) package 97% fat-free yellow cake mix
    3 egg whites
    1 cup low-fat vanilla-flavored yogurt
    ½ cup water
    1 teaspoon ground cinnamon
    1 teaspoon pumpkin pie spice
    1 cup cereal
    1 cup grated zucchini
    Spiced Caramel Frosting (page 181)

1. Preheat the oven to 350°F.

2. In a large mixing bowl, beat the cake mix, egg whites, yogurt, water, cinnamon, and pumpkin pie spice with an electric mixer at low speed until blended. Increase the speed to high and beat for 2 minutes. Stir in the cereal and zucchini. Pour the batter into 2 (9-inch) round cake pans coated with vegetable cooking spray.

3. Bake for 25 to 35 minutes, or until a wooden toothpick inserted in the center comes out clean. Cool in the pans for 10 minutes; remove from the pans and cool completely on a wire rack. Frost the cake with Spiced Caramel Frosting.

Yield: one 9-inch, 2-layer cake

Spiced Caramel Frosting

1½ cups firmly packed dark brown sugar

½ cup water

2 teaspoons espresso or coffee powder

1 teaspoon ground cinnamon

⅛ teaspoon salt

3 egg whites

¼ teaspoon cream of tartar

1. Bring the brown sugar, water, and espresso to a boil in a heavy 2-quart saucepan over medium-high heat, stirring constantly until the sugar dissolves. Cook, stirring often, until a candy thermometer reads 240°F or a ball of mixture holds together when a small amount is dropped into ice water. Remove from the heat and stir in the cinnamon and salt. Set aside.

2. Beat the egg whites and cream of tartar with an electric mixer on medium speed until foamy. Gradually add the hot sugar syrup in a slow thin stream, beating constantly until stiff peaks form and the mixture is cool.

Yield: 4 cups, or enough frosting for one 2-layer cake

Better-Than-Bread Pudding

Any granola—with or without fruit—makes this pudding heartier and more nutritious than one that uses regular day-old bread, but it still has that wonderful old-fashioned flavor. Use Quaker Sun Country Granolas, 100% Natural Granolas; C.W. Post Hearty Granola; Kellogg's Low Fat Granolas; General Mills Nature Valley Low Fat Fruit Granola.

1½ cups milk

2 large eggs

3 tablespoons butter or margarine, melted

½ cup sugar

2 teaspoons vanilla extract

3 cups cereal

1. Preheat the oven to 325°F.

2. Generously butter a 9 x 5 x 3-inch loaf pan. Whisk the milk, eggs, butter, sugar, and vanilla in a large bowl until blended. Stir in the cereal. Pour into the pan; bake for 40 minutes, or until set. Serve with ice cream. Sprinkle each serving with bourbon or brandy, if desired.

Yield: 6 servings

Just Right Shoofly Pie

A healthy pie? Well, healthier than most! And you can't mess it up; this rich-tasting, thick, baked meringue in a piecrust will always turn out right. It has lots of texture, and you can make it any flavor you want with cereal. There's a large list of cereal to choose from; each will give the right texture, so pick your own favorite: Post Fruit & Fibre (any flavor), Great Grains Raisin, Date, Pecan; General Mills Basic 4; Healthy Choice from Kellogg's Multi-Grain Raisins, Crunchy Oat Clusters and Almonds, Just Right Fruit & Nut, Nutri-Grain Almond Raisin; Ralston Foods Blueberry Pecan Muesli, Cranberry Walnut Muesli, Peach Pecan Muesli, Raspberry Almond Muesli.

> 2 large eggs
> 2 tablespoons liquid 60% vegetable oil spread
> 1 tablespoon vanilla extract, or 2 tablespoons bourbon or brandy
> ⅔ cup firmly packed light or dark brown sugar
> 2 tablespoons all-purpose flour
> ½ teaspoon baking powder
> 3 cups cereal
> 1 frozen 9-inch deep-dish piecrust, prebaked

1. Preheat the oven to 375°F.

2. Beat the eggs in a large bowl with a wire whisk; add the vegetable oil spread, vanilla, brown sugar, flour, and baking powder and whisk until blended. (Or process in a blender until smooth, then pour into a bowl.) Stir in the cereal; pour into the piecrust.

3. Bake on the lowest oven rack for 20 to 25 minutes, or until lightly browned and the center is just firm. Let cool. Serve warm or at room temperature with whipped cream, whipped topping, or ice cream.

Yield: one 9-inch pie

Fruit-Filled Ice-Cream Pie

Here's an ice-cream sundae that you can slice, loaded with the works. Shredded wheat cereal with jamlike filling makes this crust as tasty as the frozen layers: Kellogg's Strawberry Squares, Blueberry Squares, Apple Cinnamon Squares, Frosted Mini-Wheats; Nabisco Fruit Wheats Blueberry, Raspberry, Strawberry.

3½ cups cereal
2 cups toasted pecan pieces or peanuts
½ cup sugar
⅓ cup butter or margarine, melted
1 pint strawberry ice cream, softened
1 cup flaked coconut
1 (11.75-ounce) jar chocolate sauce
1 pint vanilla ice cream, softened
2 ripe bananas, sliced
2 cups sweetened whipped cream or thawed frozen whipped topping

1. Process the cereal in a food processor until finely shredded. Add 1 cup of the pecans, the sugar, and butter and process until the pecans are finely chopped and the mixture is well blended. Measure out and reserve ½ cup of the mixture. Press the remaining cereal mixture into the bottom of a 9-inch springform pan; set aside.

2. Spread the strawberry ice cream evenly over the crust; sprinkle with the coconut and the remaining 1 cup pecans. Drizzle with half of the chocolate sauce. Freeze 45 minutes, or until just firm.

3. Spread the vanilla ice cream evenly on top of the strawberry ice cream; top with the banana slices and drizzle with the remaining chocolate sauce. Top with the whipped cream; sprinkle with the reserved cereal mixture. Freeze until firm. Cover with plastic wrap and return to the freezer. Remove from the freezer 20 minutes before serving.

Yield: one 9-inch pie

Chocolate Oatmeal Cookie Mousse Parfaits

Kids of every age will love this light chocolate mousse layered with cookielike crumbs. The cereal that will stay crunchy in this layered dessert is Kellogg's Cracklin' Oat Bran, and it tastes like oatmeal cookies.

1 cup (6 ounces) milk-chocolate morsels
1 cup miniature marshmallows
⅓ cup whipping cream
2 teaspoons vanilla extract
1½ cups whipping cream, whipped, or 3 cups thawed
    frozen whipped topping
1½ cups cereal

1. Combine the chocolate, marshmallows, and ⅓ cup whipping cream in a heavy saucepan; cook over low heat, stirring constantly, until the chocolate melts. Cool to room temperature. Stir in the vanilla. Gently fold in the 1½ cups whipped cream.

2. Layer the mousse and cereal in stemmed glasses. Cover and freeze for at least 1 hour or up to 2 days. Let stand for 10 to 15 minutes before serving.

Yield: 4 to 6 servings

Upside-Down Blueberry Crunch Cake

Everything tastes better outdoors, especially this fresh, fruity cake. Take it to a tailgate party or a picnic, or just grab a piece and go sit on the hammock or deck. The buttery-tasting yellow cake has a terrific caramel topping made with Post Grape-Nuts or Kellogg's Bran Buds. The cake stays moist because cereal is added to the batter, too. If fresh blueberries are not available to go under the crunch topping, substitute drained canned pineapple chunks or drained canned or fresh pitted sweet cherries. To sift flour easily, place it in a fine wire-mesh sieve and sift over a bowl. Then measure it.

¼ cup plus 2 tablespoons butter or margarine
¼ cup firmly packed brown sugar
2 tablespoons honey
½ cup plus ⅓ cup cereal
¼ cup flaked coconut (optional)
1½ cups fresh blueberries
⅔ cup sifted all-purpose flour
1 teaspoon baking powder
¼ teaspoon salt
2 egg whites
⅔ cup sugar
2 large eggs
1½ teaspoons vanilla extract

1. Preheat the oven to 350°F.

2. Cook the butter, brown sugar, and honey together in a small saucepan, stirring constantly, until melted. Remove from the heat; let cool. Stir in ½ cup of the cereal and the coconut, if desired. Spread the mixture evenly in a greased 9-inch square baking pan. Arrange the blueberries over the mixture.

3. Combine the remaining ⅓ cup cereal, the flour, baking powder, and salt in a food processor or blender; process until finely ground. Beat the egg whites in a large mixing bowl until soft peaks form. Gradually add ⅓ cup of the sugar, beating until stiff and glossy. In a separate large mixing bowl, beat the whole eggs, vanilla, and the remaining ⅓ cup sugar until pale and thick. Whisk one-fourth of the beaten egg whites into the egg mixture; sprinkle half of the flour mixture over and fold in gently. Fold in the remaining egg whites and flour mixture.

4. Spread the batter evenly over the blueberries; bake for 30 to 35 minutes, or until a wooden toothpick inserted in the center comes out clean. Let cool in the pan for 5 minutes; invert onto a cake plate and serve warm or at room temperature.

Yield: 8 to 10 servings

Apple Praline
Oatmeal Crisp Pie

*This apple pie is a holiday necessity. If you have to take **anything** to a dinner party, volunteer for dessert and take this double-crust pie topped with rich caramel and toasted almonds. These cereals will make a crisp, sweet homemade pastry: Kellogg's Nut & Honey Crunch; General Mills Oatmeal Crisp Almond; Quaker Toasted Oatmeal Honey Nut; Post Honey Bunches of Oats.*

2 cups cereal

1⅔ cups all-purpose flour

¼ teaspoon salt

⅔ cup chilled butter or margarine, cut into pieces

¼ cup water

¾ cup sugar

2½ tablespoons cornstarch

1½ teaspoons apple pie spice

6 cups peeled, sliced tart apples (4 to 5 Granny Smith apples)

3 tablespoons commercial caramel topping

3 tablespoons toasted slivered almonds

1. Preheat the oven to 425°F.

2. Place the cereal in a food processor and process until finely crushed. Add the flour and salt; process until blended. Sprinkle the butter pieces over the cereal mixture; pulse until the mixture resembles coarse crumbs. Add the water and pulse until the dough holds together.

3. Roll out two-thirds of the dough between 2 pieces of plastic wrap to an 11-inch circle. Fit into a lightly greased 9-inch pie plate. Roll out the remaining dough into a 10-inch circle between 2 pieces of plastic wrap; refrigerate.

4. Combine the sugar, cornstarch, and apple pie spice in a large bowl; add the apples and toss until well mixed. Spoon into the pastry shell; fit the top crust over the apples. Trim and flute the edges, pressing together to seal. Prick the top crust with a fork 6 times. Cover the edges of the piecrust with aluminum foil. Bake for 20 minutes; remove from the oven and discard the foil. Reduce the oven temperature to 350°F and bake for an additional 30 minutes, or until golden brown. Remove from the oven. Drizzle with the caramel topping and sprinkle with the almonds. Serve warm or cold.

Yield: one 9-inch pie

Frosty Fruit Salad with Oats and Honey

Versions of this dessertlike, frozen cream and fruit salad often made with sour cream, mayonnaise, cream, and lots of pecans, have graced Southern sideboards since home freezers were invented. It makes a wonderful light ending to a summer meal, or serve as a salad on lettuce leaves with grilled meats. You'll think you're eating sherbet with fruit in it. We've reduced the fat by using light sour cream and replacing the nuts with granola without fruit: Kellogg's Low Fat Granola without Raisins; Quaker Sun Country Granola with Almonds, 100% Natural Granola Oats & Honey. (If you freeze granolas with fruit, the fruits freeze so hard they will break your teeth.)

> 1 (15¼-ounce) can crushed pineapple
> 2 (16-ounce) cartons plus 1 (8-ounce) carton light sour cream
> 1 cup evaporated skim milk
> 2¼ cups sugar
> ¼ teaspoon salt
> 1½ cups cereal
> 1½ cups miniature marshmallows
> ½ cup chopped maraschino cherries
> 2 small ripe bananas, peeled and diced

1. Drain the pineapple, reserving the juice. Measure out ⅓ cup juice for this recipe. In a large bowl, whisk together the sour cream, milk, sugar, salt, and pineapple juice. Stir in the pineapple, cereal, marshmallows, cherries, and bananas. Pour into a 13 x 9 x 2-inch baking pan; cover with foil and freeze overnight.

2. Remove from the freezer only long enough to cut into squares. Return to the freezer until ready to serve.

Yield: 18 servings

RECIPE REFERENCE LIST

General Mills

Apple Cinnamon Cheerios: Fruity Party Chow 18, Apple Cinnamon Cheesecake 163

Basic 4: Frosted Almond Raisin Carrot Cookies 47, Just Right Shoofly Pie 183, The Complete Breakfast Pizza 81, Ultimate Carrot Cake 132

Berry Berry Kix: Fruity Party Chow 18, Banana Shake Cereal 105, Strawberry Shake Cereal 105

Boo Berry: Fruity Party Chow 18

Cheerios: Shake-a-Snack 18, All-My-Favorite-Things Gorp 23, Jessie Kate's Chocolate Shake 19, Chocolate Caramel-Nut Dessert Mix 25, Caribbean Chips 22, Wow, I Could Have Had a Lemonade Cereal 105, Honey and Spice Cocktail Crunch 14

Cinnamon Toast Crunch: Banana Crunch Pudding 4, Double Dip Banana Pudding 150

Clusters: Rocky Road Clusters Fudge 41, Chocolate Chip Banana Crunch Muffins 76, Warm Apple Crisp 171

Cocoa Puffs: Cereal Snowmen 141, Cocoa Cookie Dirt Cups 142, Wow, I Could Have Had a Lemonade Cereal 105, The Scariest Halloween Spook Hands 140

Count Chocula: Fruity Party Chow 18

Country Corn Flakes: Mexican Turkey Burgers 87, Flaky 4-Ingredient Honey Mustard Chicken 90, Lighter-Than-Average Crab Cakes 113, Crunchy Peanut Thai Pasta 116, Special Turkey Meatballs 113, Savory Chili Ranch Cheesecake 114, Commonsense Country Oat Squash Casserole 86, Unfried Green Tomatoes, Etc. 88, Toasty Fried Cheese Marinara 89, Totally Spicy Hot Wings 91, Captain Hook's Fish Sticks 151, King of Crunch Tenders 92, Candy Cornflake Wreaths 139

Fiber One: Blender Lunch Box Bran Muffins 101, Hearty Bran Nut Bread 82, Bran Gingerbread 79

Frankenberry: Fruity Party Chow 18

Frosted Cheerios: Fruity Party Chow 18, Banana Shake Cereal 105, Strawberry Shake Cereal 105, Oranges and Cream Cereal 105

Golden Grahams: Magic Chocolate Cereal Bars 28, Caramel Graham Squares 30, S'More Brownie Torte 158, No-Bake Golden Cherry Almond Pie 162, Key Lime Cheesecake with Butter Graham Crust 160, Gooey Butterscotch Cereal Bars 32, All-My-Favorite-Things Gorp 23

Honey Frosted Wheaties: Baked Honey Apples 143

Honey Nut Cheerios: All-My-Favorite-Things Gorp 23, Tunnel of Fudge Brownie Tarts 156, Vanilla Nut Biscotti 49, Key Lime Cheesecake with Butter Graham Crust 160

Kix: Pucker Up Lemon Squares 29, Nutty Buddies 31, Honey and Spice Cocktail Crunch 14, Jessie Kate's Chocolate Shake 19, Cereal Snowmen 141, Gobblin' Caramel Puff Balls 138, Wow, I Could Have Had a Lemonade Cereal 105, Mock Apple Pie 174

Lucky Charms: Fruity Party Chow 18

Multi-Grain Cheerios: Tunnel of Fudge Brownie Tarts 156

Nature Valley Low Fat Fruit Granola: Granola Biker Bars 37, Better-Than-Bread Pudding 182

Oatmeal Crisp: Margaritaville Cereal 105

Oatmeal Crisp Almond: Almond Praline Oatmeal Crisp Pie 188, Honey Almond Fruit Crumble with Sweet Lemon Cream 178, White Chocolate Macaroons 42, Design Your Own Monster Cookies 44, Carrot Cake Temptation Muffins and Cupcakes 74, Quick Peanut Butter and Jelly Oatmeal Crisp Cookies 9, The Quickest Peanut Butter Oatmeal "Cookie" 136, Caramel Clusters 137, Warm Apple Crisp 171

Raisin Nut Bran: Rocky Road Clusters Fudge 41, Quick Raisin and Nut Energy Bars 39

Reese's Peanut Butter Puffs: Cereal Snowmen 141, Gobblin' Caramel Puff Balls 138, Cocoa Cookie Dirt Cups 142, PBJ Shake Cereal 105

S'Mores Grahams: Caramel Graham Squares 30

Sun Crunchers: Warm Apple Crisp 171

Total Corn Flakes: Bakery Glazed Cinnamon Raisin Biscuits 119, Mexican Turkey Burgers 87, Unfried Green Tomatoes, Etc. 88, Flaky 4-Ingredient Honey Mustard Chicken 90, Lighter-Than-Average Crab Cakes 112, Crunchy Peanut Thai Pasta 116, Special Turkey Meatballs 113, Savory Chili Ranch Cheesecake 114, Commonsense Country Oat Squash Casserole 86, Toasty Fried Cheese Marinara 89, King of Crunch Tenders 92, Candy Cornflake Wreaths 139, Totally Spicy Hot Wings 91, All-Purpose Crunchy Topping 109

Trix: Fruity Party Chow 18, Cereal Snowmen 141, Banana Shake Cereal 105, Strawberry Shake Cereal 105

Wheaties: Bakery Glazed Cinnamon Raisin Biscuits 119, Crunchy Peanut Thai Pasta 116, 100% Brunch in a Casserole 60, Savory Chili Ranch Cheesecake 114, Ham and Cheese Wheat Brunchwich 61, Commonsense Country Oat Squash Casserole 86, Sweet Wheaty Onion Pie 118, Sunday Morning Nutty Waffles 54, Breakfast in a Muffin 53

Wheaties Honey Gold: Ham and Cheese Wheat Brunchwich 61, Candy Cornflake Wreaths 139, Berry Toaster Pastry Muffins 146

Whole Grain Total: Crunchy Peanut Thai Pasta 116, Bakery Glazed Cinnamon Raisin Biscuits 119, Savory Chili Ranch Cheesecake 114, 100% Brunch in a Casserole 60, Ham and Cheese Wheat Brunchwich 61, Commonsense Country Oat Squash Casserole 86, Sweet Wheaty Onion Pie 118, Totally Spicy Hot Wings 91, Sunday Morning Nutty Waffles 54, Breakfast in a Muffin 53, All-Purpose Crunchy Topping 109

Kellogg's

All-Bran: Hearty Bran Nut Bread 82, Blender Lunch Box Bran Muffins 101, Bran-Nutty Cheese Balls 8, Bran Gingerbread 79

All-Bran Extra Fiber: Hearty Bran Nut Bread 82

Apple Cinnamon Rice Krispies: Gobblin' Caramel Puff Balls 138, Crispy Character Cake 144

Apple Cinnamon Squares: Fruit-Filled Ice-Cream Pie 184, Apple Cinnamon Cheesecake 163

Apple Jacks: Fruity Party Chow 18, Banana Shake Cereal 105, Strawberry Shake Cereal 105

Blueberry Squares: Fruit-Filled Ice-Cream Pie 184

Bran Buds: Upside-Down Blueberry Crunch Cake 186, Bran-Nutty Cheese Balls 8, Budding Peach Pie 168

Cocoa Krispies: Chocolate Nougat Crispy Bars 36, Easy Chocolate Crispy Bar 7, Chocolate Crunch Cups 137, Chocolate Crunch Bars 148, Special Cereal Treats 134, Crispy Character Cake 144, Crispy Crust Fudge Raspberry Tart 164, Cocoa Crispy Candy 172

Common Sense Oat Bran: Commonsense Country Oat Squash Casserole 86, Sweet Wheaty Onion Pie 118, Sunday Morning Nutty Waffles 54, Peanut Butter Snack Bars 145, Breakfast in a Muffin 53

Complete Bran Flakes: Bakery Glazed Cinnamon Raisin Biscuits 119, 100% Brunch in a Casserole 60, Savory Chili Ranch Cheesecake 114, Sweet Wheaty Onion Pie 118, Sunday Morning Nutty Waffles 54, Peanut Butter Snack Bars 145, Breakfast in a Muffin 53

Corn Flakes: Bakery Glazed Cinnamon Raisin Biscuits 119, Flaky 4-Ingredient Honey Mustard Chicken 90, Lighter-Than-Average Crab Cakes 112, Crunchy Peanut Thai Pasta 116, Special Turkey Meatballs 113, Savory Chili Ranch Cheesecake 114, Commonsense Country Oat Squash Casserole 86, Totally Spicy Hot Wings 91, Captain Hook's Fish Sticks 151, Candy Cornflake Wreaths 139, King of Crunch Tenders 92, Mexican Turkey Burgers 87

Corn Pops: Mock Apple Pie 174, Nutty Buddies 31, Honey and Spice Cocktail Crunch 14, Candy Tin Snack Mix 17, Caribbean Chips 22, Gobblin' Caramel Puff Balls 138, Caramel Clusters 137, Wow, I Could Have Had a Lemonade Cereal 105, Chewy Chocolate Peanut Clusters 173

Cracklin' Oat Bran: Double Blueberry Morning Muffins 78, Banana Split Pie 159, Crisp-Layered Neapolitan 170, Chocolate Oatmeal Cookie Mousse Parfaits 185, Frozen Crackling Cappuccino Ice-Cream Dessert 106, Lemon Blueberry Bran Bread 80

Crispix: Crispy Crust Tuna Family Supper 94, Chicken Nacho Supper in a Bowl 95, Chèvre and Wild Rice Stuffed "Porcupine" Chicken 120, Italian Seasoned Roasted Vegetables 97, All-My-Favorite-Things Gorp 23, Chocolate Caramel-Nut Dessert Mix 25, Shake-a-Snack 18, Curly Taco Snack Mix 15, Cheesy Mustard Snack Mix 16, South American Mole Mix 13, Oriental Chow Mix 24, Mediterranean Munchies 20, Italian Munchies 20, Cowboy Caviar 21, Crush-to-Smithereens Chicken 149

Double Dip Crunch: Banana Crunch Pudding 4, Double Dip Banana Pudding 150

Froot Loops: Fruity Party Chow 18, Banana Shake Cereal 105, Strawberry Shake Cereal 105

Frosted Flakes: Banana Shake Cereal 105, Strawberry Shake Cereal 105

Frosted Mini-Wheats: Frosted Streusel French Toast 66, Frosted Wheat Pastry Twists 72, Haystack Brownie Sundaes 166, Pear Baklava Torte 176, Fruit-Filled Ice-Cream Pie 184

Frosted Mini-Wheats Bite Size: Frosted Streusel French Toast 66, Frosted Wheat Pastry Twists 72, Haystack Brownie Sundaes 166

Frosted Rice Krispies: Chocolate Nougat Crispy Bars 36, Easy Chocolate Crispy Bar 7, Crispy Character Cake 144

Fruitful Bran: Overnight Refrigerator Grain Pancakes 59

Fruity Marshmallow Krispies: Crispy Character Cake 144

Healthy Choice from Kellogg's Multi-Grain Flakes: Berry Toaster Pastry Muffins 146

Healthy Choice from Kellogg's Multi-Grain Raisins, Crunchy Oat Clusters and Almonds: Just Right Shoofly Pie 183

Healthy Choice from Kellogg's Multi-Grain Squares: Indian Curry Snacks 12, Frosted Streusel French Toast 66, Lemon Shredded Coffee Cake 69, Frosted Wheat Pastry Twists 72

Just Right Fruit & Nut: Frosted Almond Raisin Carrot Cookies 47, Just Right Shoofly Pie 183, Ultimate Carrot Cake 132, Maple Sweet Potato Gratin 128

Just Right with Crunchy Nuggets: Quick Raisin and Nut Energy Bars 39, Maple Sweet Potato Gratin 128

Kellogg's Product 19: Flaky 4-Ingredient Honey Mustard Chicken 90, Savory Chili Ranch Cheesecake 114

Low Fat Granola with Raisins: Granola Biker Bars 37, Better-Than-Bread Pudding 182

Low Fat Granola Without Raisins: Magic Chocolate Cereal Bars 28, Granola Blondies 38, Better-Than-Bread Pudding 182, Chocolate Granola Fruit Drops 6, Red, White, and Blue Granola Parfait 83, Pear Streusel Acorn Squash 100, Granola Wedding Cookies 43, 100% Natural Scalloped Apples 127, Frosty Fruit Salad with Oats and Honey 190

Müeslix Crispy Blend: Quick Raisin and Nut Energy Bars 39, Fruit and Grain Zucchini Spice Cake 180, Maple Sweet Potato Gratin 128

Müeslix Crispy Blend Apple & Almond Crunch: Apple Date Crunch Bars 40, Maple Sweet Potato Gratin 128

Müeslix Golden Crunch: Fruit and Grain Zucchini Spice Cake 180, Maple Sweet Potato Gratin 128

Müeslix Raisin & Almond Crunch with Dates: Frosted Almond Raisin Carrot Cookies 47, Maple Sweet Potato Gratin 128, Ultimate Carrot Cake 132

Nut & Honey Crunch: Design Your Own Monster Cookies 44, Carrot Cake Temptation Muffins and Cupcakes 74, Caramel Clusters 137, Baked Honey Apples 143, Apple Praline Oatmeal Crisp Pie 188, Warm Apple Crisp 171

Nut & Honey Crunch O's: Tunnel of Fudge Brownie Tarts 156, Key Lime Cheesecake with Butter Graham Crust 160, Vanilla Nut Biscotti 49

Nutri-Grain Almond Raisin: Frosted Almond Raisin Carrot Cookies 47, Quick Raisin and Nut Energy Bars 39, Just Right Shoofly Pie 183, Maple Sweet Potato Gratin 128, Ultimate Carrot Cake 132

Nutri-Grain Golden Wheat: Fruit and Grain Zucchini Spice Cake 180, Maple Sweet Potato Gratin 128

Nutri-Grain Golden Wheat and Raisin: Maple Sweet Potato Gratin 128

Pop-Tarts Crunch Frosted Brown Sugar Cinnamon: Cheesecake Fruit Tart 155

Pop-Tarts Crunch Frosted Strawberry: Strawberries and Cream Dessert 150, Cheesecake Fruit Tart 155

Raisin Bran: Raisin Bran Brunch Muffins 56, Spice Muffins 57, Pineapple Muffins 57, Fruit Cocktail Muffins 57, Chocolate Chip Muffins 57, Apple Muffins 57, Overnight Refrigerator Grain Pancakes 59

Rice Krispies: Pucker Up Lemon Squares 29, Chocolate Nougat Crispy Bars 36, Easy Chocolate Crispy Bar 7, Gobblin' Caramel Puff Balls 138, Chocolate Crunch Cups 137, Caramel Clusters 137, Chocolate Crunch Bars 148,

Special Cereal Treats 134, Crispy Character Cake 144, Crispy Crust Fudge Raspberry Tart 164, Chocolate Chip Cookie Pizza 167

Rice Krispies Treats: Peanut Chocolate Chip Crispies 135

Smacks: Candy Tin Snack Mix 17, Gobblin' Caramel Puff Balls 138, Chewy Chocolate Peanut Clusters 173

Special K: Aunt Cora's Special Cookies 10, Special Turkey Meatballs 113, Savory Chili Ranch Cheesecake 114, Sweet Wheaty Onion Pie 118, Breakfast in a Muffin 53

Strawberry Squares: Fruit-Filled Ice-Cream Pie 184

Temptations French Vanilla Almond: White Chocolate Almond Bars 33, White Chocolate Macaroons 42, Carrot Cake Temptation Muffins and Cupcakes 74, Caramel Clusters 137, Tropical Fruit and Nut Crisp 157, Warm Apple Crisp 171

Temptations Honey Roasted Pecan: Honey-Roasted Pecan Fudge Bars 35, Carrot Cake Temptation Muffins and Cupcakes 74, Tropical Fruit and Nut Crisp 157, Warm Apple Crisp 171

Toasted Corn Flakes: Mexican Turkey Burgers 87, Flaky 4-Ingredient Honey Mustard Chicken 90, Crunchy Peanut Thai Pasta 116, Savory Chili Ranch Cheesecake 114, Commonsense Country Oat Squash Casserole 86, Unfried Green Tomatoes, Etc. 88, Toasty Fried Cheese Marinara 89, Totally Spicy Hot Wings 91, All-Purpose Crunchy Topping 109

Nabisco

Frosted Wheat Bites: Frosted Streusel French Toast 66, Frosted Wheat Pastry Twists 72, Frosted "Coconut" Pie 161, Haystack Brownie Sundaes 166

Fruit Wheats Blueberry: Fruit-Filled Ice-Cream Pie 184

Fruit Wheats Raspberry: Fruit-Filled Ice-Cream Pie 184

Fruit Wheats Strawberry: Fruit-Filled Ice-Cream Pie 184

Shredded Wheat: Oven Crusted Potatoes 99, Tuscan Shredded Wheat Bread 70, Lemon Shredded Coffee Cake 69, Crispy Cheese Puffs 72, Garlic Shred Croutons 108, Curried Walnut Wheat Burgers 125

Shredded Wheat 'N Bran: Oriental Chow Mix 24, Mediterranean Munchies 20, Italian Munchies 20, Oven Crusted Potatoes 99, Tuscan Shredded Wheat Bread 70, Lemon Shredded Coffee Cake 69, Garlic Shred Croutons 108, Curried Walnut Wheat Burgers 125, Cheesy Mustard Snack Mix 16

Shredded Wheat Spoon Size: Curly Taco Snack Mix 15, Cheesy Mustard Snack Mix 16, Indian Curry Snacks 12, Oriental Chow Mix 24, Mediterranean Munchies 20, Italian Munchies 20, Oven Crusted Potatoes 99, Tuscan Shredded Wheat Bread 70, Coconut Shrimp Almondine 124, Lemon Shredded Coffee Cake 69, Crispy Cheese Puffs 72, Garlic Shred Croutons 108, Curried Walnut Wheat Burgers 125

Team Flakes: Captain Hook's Fish Sticks 151

100% Bran: Blender Lunch Box Bran Muffins 101, Bran-Nutty Cheese Balls 8, Hearty Bran Nut Bread 82, Bran Gingerbread 79

Post

Banana Nut Crunch: Hawaiian Banana Banana Bread 73, Chocolate Chip Banana Crunch Muffins 76, Banana Crunch Pudding 4, Tropical Fruit and Nut Crisp 157, Banana Shake Cereal 105, Strawberry Shake Cereal 105, Tropical Quencher Cereal 105, Double Dip Banana Pudding 150

Blueberry Morning: Red, White, and Blue Granola Parfait 83, Banana Shake Cereal 105, Strawberry Shake Cereal 105, Double Blueberry Morning Muffins 78

Bran Flakes: Bakery Glazed Cinnamon Raisin Biscuits 119, 100% Brunch in a Casserole 60, Sweet Wheaty Onion Pie 118, Sunday Morning Nutty Waffles 54, Peanut Butter Snack Bars 145, Breakfast in a Muffin 53

C. W. Post Hearty Granola: Granola Biker Bars 37, Better-Than-Bread Pudding 182

Fruit & Fibre (any flavor): Just Right Shoofly Pie 183

Fruit & Fibre Dates, Raisins, Walnuts: Frosted Almond Raisin Carrot Cookies 47, Ultimate Carrot Cake 132, Maple Sweet Potato Gratin 128

Golden Crisp: Gobblin' Caramel Puff Balls 138, Chewy Chocolate Peanut Clusters 173

Grape-Nuts: Upside-Down Blueberry Crunch Cake 186, Bran-Nutty Cheese Balls 8, Budding Peach Pie 168

Grape-Nuts Flakes: Bakery Glazed Cinnamon Raisin Biscuits 119, 100% Brunch in a Casserole 60, Sunday Morning Nutty Waffles 54, Peanut Butter Snack Bars 145

Great Grains Crunchy Pecan: Cranberry Whole-Grain Nut Bars 34, Quick Raisin and Nut Energy Bars 39, Pecan Chicken Burgers 126, The Complete Breakfast Pizza 81, Maple Sweet Potato Gratin 128

Great Grains Raisin, Date, Pecan: Frosted Almond Raisin Carrot Cookies 47, Quick Raisin and Nut Energy Bars 39, Just Right Shoofly Pie 183, Ultimate Carrot Cake 132, Maple Sweet Potato Gratin 128

Honey Bunches of Oats: Rocky Road Clusters Fudge 41, Design Your Own Monster Cookies 44, Chocolate Chip Banana Crunch Muffins 76, Caramel Clusters 137, Baked Honey Apples 143, Apple Praline Oatmeal Crisp Pie 188, Warm Apple Crisp 171

Honey Bunches of Oats with Almonds: Carrot Cake Temptation Muffins and Cupcakes 74, Honey Almond Fruit Crumble with Sweet Lemon Cream 178, Warm Apple Crisp 171

Honeycomb: Wow, I Could Have Had a Lemonade Cereal 105, Vanilla Nut Biscotti 49

Post Toasties: Mexican Turkey Burgers 87, Flaky 4-Ingredient Honey Mustard Chicken 90, Lighter-Than-Average Crab Cakes 113, Crunchy Peanut Thai Pasta 116, Savory Chili Ranch Cheesecake 114, Commonsense Country Oat Squash Casserole 86, Captain Hook's Fish Sticks 151, Peanut Butter Snack Bars 145, King of Crunch Tenders 92, Special Turkey Meatballs 113

Waffle Crisp: Pucker Up Lemon Squares 29, Candy Tin Snack Mix 17, Jessie Kate's Chocolate Shake 19, Chocolate Ice-Cream Cones 5, Banana Cereal Split 106, Sunday Morning Nutty Waffles 54

Quaker Oats

Cap'n Crunch: Candy Tin Snack Mix 17, Chocolate Ice-Cream Cones 5, King of Crunch Tenders 92, Chewy Chocolate Peanut Clusters 173, Mock Apple Pie 174

Cap'n Crunch's Deep Sea Crunch: Candy Tin Snack Mix 17

Cap'n Crunch's Peanut Butter Crunch: PBJ Shake Cereal 105, Chewy Chocolate Peanut Clusters 173

Cinnamon Life: Cranberry Pineapple Crunch Casserole 106, Country Apple Pudding 68

Crunchy Corn Bran: Chicken Nacho Supper in a Bowl 95, Battered Chicken Salad 122, Shake-a-Snack 18, Curly Taco Snack Mix 15, South American Mole Mix 13, Indian Curry Snacks 12, Oriental Chow Mix 24, Crush-to-Smithereens Chicken 149

Life: Cranberry Pineapple Crunch Casserole 106, Honey and Spice Cocktail Crunch 14, Country Apple Pudding 68

Popeye Jeepers Crispy Corn Puffs: Mock Apple Pie 174

Popeye Sweet Crunch: Candy Tin Snack Mix 17

Quaker Oat Bran: Cranberry Pineapple Crunch Casserole 106, Indian Curry Snacks 12, Country Apple Pudding 68

Quaker OH's—Honey Graham: Key Lime Cheesecake with Butter Graham Crust 160, No-Bake Golden Cherry Almond Pie 162, Vanilla Nut Biscotti 49

Quaker Toasted Oatmeal Squares: Battered Chicken Salad 122, All-My-Favorite-Things Gorp 23, Jessie Kate's Chocolate Shake 19, Honey and Spice Cocktail Crunch 14, Indian Curry Snacks 12, Caribbean Chips 22

Sun Country Granola—Raisin and Date: Granola Biker Bars 37, Better-Than-Bread Pudding 182

Sun Country Granola with Almonds: Magic Chocolate Cereal Bars 28, Granola Wedding Cookies 43, Granola Blondies 38, 100% Natural Scalloped Apples 127, Better-Than-Bread Pudding 182, Red, White, and Blue Granola Parfait 83, Chocolate Granola Fruit Drops 6, Pear Streusel Acorn Squash 100, Frosty Fruit Salad with Oats and Honey 190

Toasted Oatmeal: Design Your Own Monster Cookies 44, Caramel Clusters 137, Quick Peanut Butter and Jelly Oatmeal Crisp Cookies 9, The Quickest Peanut Butter Oatmeal "Cookie" 136, Margaritaville Cereal 105, Double Chocolate Chip Cookie Chocolate Chip Cookies 46

Toasted Oatmeal Honey Nut: Design Your Own Monster Cookies 44, Carrot Cake Temptation Muffins and Cupcakes 74, Honey Almond Fruit Crumble with Sweet Lemon Cream 178, Apple Praline Oatmeal Crisp Pie 188, Baked Honey Apples 143, Warm Apple Crisp 171

Toasted Oatmeal with Almonds: Rocky Road Clusters Fudge 41, Warm Apple Crisp 171

100% Natural Granola Oats & Honey: Granola Wedding Cookies 43, Granola Biker Bars 37, Granola Blondies 38, 100% Natural Scalloped Apples 127, Frosty Fruit Salad with Oats and Honey 190, Chocolate Granola Fruit Drops 6, Red, White, and Blue Granola Parfait 83, Pear Streusel Acorn Squash 100, Magic Chocolate Cereal Bars 28, Better-Than-Bread Pudding 182

100% Natural Low Fat Granola with Raisins: Granola Biker Bars 37

100% Natural Oats, Honey, & Raisins: Better-Than-Bread Pudding 182, Granola Biker Bars 37

Ralston Foods

Almond Delight: Warm Apple Crisp 171, White Chocolate Almond Bars 33, Honey Almond Fruit Crumble with Sweet Lemon Cream 178

Blueberry Pecan Muesli: Cranberry Whole-Grain Nut Bars 34, Just Right Shoofly Pie 183, Banana Shake Cereal 105, Strawberry Shake Cereal 105

Cookie-Crisp: Double Chocolate Chip Cookie Chocolate Chip Cookies 46, Chocolate Ice-Cream Cones 5, Cookies and Cream Pie 107, Cocoa Cookie Dirt Cups 142

Corn Chex: Crispy Crust Tuna Family Supper 94, Creamy Double Corn Casserole 96, Chicken Nacho Supper in a Bowl 95, Chèvre and Wild Rice Stuffed "Porcupine" Chicken 120, Crispy Cheese Wafers 98, Italian Seasoned Roasted Vegetables 97, All-My-Favorite-Things Gorp 23, Jessie Kate's Chocolate Shake 19, Chocolate Caramel-Nut Dessert Mix 25, Shake-a-Snack 18, Curly Taco Snack Mix 15, Cheesy Mustard Snack Mix 16, South American Mole Mix 13, Oriental Chow Mix 24, Mediterranean Munchies 20, Italian Munchies 20, Cowboy Caviar 21, Caribbean Chips 22, Crush-to-Smithereens Chicken 149

Cranberry Walnut Muesli: Cranberry Whole-Grain Nut Bars 34, Just Right Shoofly Pie 183, Banana Shake Cereal 105, Strawberry Shake Cereal 105

Double Chex: Crispy Crust Tuna Family Supper 94, Chicken Nacho Supper in a Bowl 95, Chèvre and Wild Rice Stuffed "Porcupine" Chicken 120, Italian Seasoned Roasted Vegetables 97, Shake-a-Snack 18, All-My-Favorite-Things Gorp 23, Chocolate Caramel-Nut Dessert Mix 25, Curly Taco Snack Mix 15, Cheesy Mustard Snack Mix 16, South American Mole Mix 13, Oriental Chow Mix 24, Mediterranean Munchies 20, Italian Munchies 20, Cowboy Caviar 21, Caribbean Chips 22, Crush-to-Smithereens Chicken 149

Graham Chex: Magic Chocolate Cereal Bars 28, Caramel Graham Squares 30, Gooey Butterscotch Cereal Bars 32, All-My-Favorite-Things Gorp 23, Caribbean Chips 22, Jessie Kate's Chocolate Shake 19, S'More Brownie Torte 158, No-Bake Golden Cherry Almond Pie 162

Multi Bran Chex: Gooey Butterscotch Cereal Bars 32, Crispy Crust Tuna Family Supper 94, Quick Whole Wheat Bread 67, Crispy Cheese Wafers 98, Wheat Grain Black Bean Burgers 93, Pumpkin Wheat Muffins 64, Shake-a-Snack 18, All-My-Favorite-Things Gorp 23, Jessie Kate's Chocolate Shake 19, Curly Taco Snack Mix 15, Cheesy Mustard Snack Mix 16, South American Mole Mix 13, Indian Curry Snacks 12, Oriental Chow Mix 24, Mediterranean Munchies 20, Italian Munchies 20, Cowboy Caviar 21, Caribbean Chips 22

Peach Pecan Muesli: Just Right Shoofly Pie 183, Banana Shake Cereal 105, Strawberry Shake Cereal 105

Raspberry Almond Muesli: Just Right Shoofly Pie 183, Banana Shake Cereal 105, Strawberry Shake Cereal 105

Rice Chex: Gooey Butterscotch Cereal Bars 32, Crispy Crust Tuna Family Supper 94, All-My-Favorite-Things Gorp 23, Jessie Kate's Chocolate Shake 19, Chocolate Caramel-Nut Dessert Mix 25, Shake-a-Snack 18, Curly Taco Snack Mix 15, Cheesy Mustard Snack Mix 16, South American Mole Mix 13, Indian Curry Snacks 12, Oriental Chow Mix 24, Mediterranean Munchies 20, Italian Munchies 20, Cowboy Caviar 21, Caribbean Chips 22

Strawberry Pecan Muesli: Banana Shake Cereal 105, Strawberry Shake Cereal 105

100% Whole Grain Wheat Chex: Crispy Crust Tuna Family Supper 94, Buttermilk Wheat Biscuits or Crackers 62, Quick Whole Wheat Bread 67, Crispy Cheese Wafers 98, Wheat Grain Black Bean Burgers 93, Pumpkin Wheat Muffins 64, Shake-a-Snack 18, Jessie Kate's Chocolate Shake 19, All-My-Favorite-Things Gorp 23, Curly Taco Snack Mix 15, Cheesy Mustard Snack Mix 16, South American Mole Mix 13, Indian Curry Snacks 12, Oriental Chow Mix 24, Mediterranean Munchies 20, Italian Munchies 20, Cowboy Caviar 21

INDEX

About the Author

DEBBY MAUGANS is the owner of Southern Food Consultants based in Birmingham, Alabama. In addition to developing recipes for *Cooking Light, Shape, Southern Living,* and *Health* magazines, she developed the recipes for Fannie Flagg's *The Whistle Stop Cafe Cookbook,* the Kenneth Cooper Institute's *Guilt-Free Comfort Food,* and the Southern Living Cooking School cookbooks. Her recipes have also appeared in *The American Health Cookbook, Cooking Light Cookbooks 1993, 1994, 1995, Holidays & Celebrations, Light & Luscious, Quick & Healthy, The Low-Fat, High Flavor Cookbook,* and *Heart Healthy One-Dish Meals.* She also styles food for film productions and for still photography.

Debby crunches cereal with her 10-year-old daughter, Jessie Kate, every morning, and both of them take their milk on the side, not in the bowl. JK gets marshmallows in hers, and Debby prefers a few chocolate morsels. Oreo the cat likes whatever falls from their spoons.